I0794794

STUDY GUIDE

Knowing Scripture

R.C. Sproul

LIGONIER MINISTRIES
Renew your Mind.
LIGONIER.ORG | 800-435-4343

421 Ligonier Court, Sanford, FL 32771
Email: info@ligonier.org

Printed in China.

Contents

Introduction

Christians need some basic guidance on how to interpret the Bible. Just a few principles of interpretation will go a long way toward helping the believer understand the Scriptures. Here are the easy-to-use skills for your own personal study. Through the course you will learn how to approach difficult passages, how to find the true meaning of each verse, and how to place each passage in its proper context. This series is sure to be helpful to all who seek to know God's revelation better. These lectures parallel Dr. Sproul's book *Knowing Scripture*.

This study guide is a companion to the video teaching series. Whether you are using the DVDs, streaming the videos on Ligonier.org, or going through the course in Ligonier Connect, this resource is designed to help you make the most of the learning experience. For each message in the series, there is a corresponding lesson in this guide. Here is what you will find in each lesson:

INTRODUCTION	The introduction is a brief paragraph that summarizes the content covered in the lecture and considered in the study guide lesson. **How to use:** Use the introduction to each lesson to get a sense of the big picture before watching the video. Refer to these statements as you work through the study guide to remind yourself of what you have already covered and where you are headed.
LEARNING GOALS	The learning goals are the knowledge and skills the study guide lesson will endeavor to equip you with as you work through the lecture content. **How to use:** Familiarize yourself with the goals of each lesson before engaging with its contents. Keeping the overall purpose in mind as you watch each video and reflect on or discuss the questions will help you get the most out of each lesson.
KEY IDEAS	The key ideas are the major points or takeaways from the lecture. **How to use:** Use these ideas to prepare yourself for each lesson and to review previous lessons. They describe specifically the knowledge each lecture is communicating.

REFLECTION & DISCUSSION QUESTIONS	The questions are the guided reflection and/or discussion component of the lesson that are intended to help you prepare for, process, and organize what you are learning. **How to use:** Reflect on individually or discuss in a group the questions in the order in which they appear in the lesson. The time stamps in the right margin indicate where the answers to questions during the video can be found.
PRAYER	The prayer section offers suggestions for how to close the lesson in prayer with respect to what was taught in the lecture. **How to use:** Consider using each lesson's prayer section as a guide to personal or group prayer. These sections follow the ACTS prayer model, which you can learn more about in R.C. Sproul's Crucial Questions booklet *Does Prayer Change Things?* This helpful guide is available as a free e-book at Ligonier.org.
REVIEW QUIZ	The review quiz is a set of six multiple-choice questions that appears at the end of each lesson. **How to use:** Use each quiz to check your comprehension and memory of the major points covered in each lecture. It will be most beneficial to your learning if you take a lesson's quiz either sometime between lessons or just before you begin the next lesson in the study guide.
ANSWER KEY	The answer key provides explanations for the reflection and discussion questions and answers to the multiple-choice questions in the review quiz. **How to use:** Use the answer key to check your own answers or when you do not know the answer. Note: Do not give in too quickly; struggling for a few moments to recall an answer reinforces it in your mind.

Study Schedules

The following table suggests four plans for working through the *Knowing Scripture* video teaching series and this companion study guide. Whether you are going through this series on your own or with a group, these schedules should help you plan your study path.

	Extended 14-Week Plan	**Standard 12-Week Plan**	**Abbreviated 6-Week Plan**	**Intensive 4-Week Plan**
Week		**Lesson**		
1	*	1	1 & 2	1–3
2	1	2	3 & 4	4–6
3	2	3	5 & 6	7–9
4	3	4	7 & 8	10–12
5	4	5	9 & 10	
6	5	6	11 & 12	
7	6	7		
8	7	8		
9	8	9		
10	9	10		
11	10	11		
12	11	12		
13	12			
14	*			

* For these weeks, rather than completing lessons, spend your time discussing and praying about your learning goals for the study (the first week) and the most valuable takeaways from the study (the last week).

1

Why Study the Bible?

INTRODUCTION

As Christians, we are *all* called to master the most important tool of the Christian life—the Bible. This calling means that we must increase our skills as interpreters of the Bible. To appreciate the importance of stretching our abilities, we must first understand why we should study the Bible. In this lesson, Dr. Sproul emphasizes the eternal significance of the Bible, God's concern that we be diligent students of His Word, and our duty to study and our privilege of studying it.

LEARNING GOALS

When you have finished this lesson, you should be able to:

- Name two common excuses why people do not study the Bible
- Understand the Bible's perspicuity as a key attribute of Scripture
- Name and support the reasons why we are to study the Bible

KEY IDEAS

- The Bible is the best-selling book of all time, yet our day is beset by biblical illiteracy.
- The basic message of the Bible concerning God and salvation is clear.
- The two basic reasons to study the Bible are our duty and privilege.

REFLECTION & DISCUSSION QUESTIONS

Before the Video

What Do You Think?

Take a moment to answer the following questions. They will prepare you for the lecture.

- Why should people study the Bible?
- What are some reasons that you've struggled to study the Bible in the past?

Scripture Reading

And these words that I command you today shall be on your heart. You shall teach them diligently to your children, and shall talk of them when you sit in your house, and when you walk by the way, and when you lie down, and when you rise. You shall bind them as a sign on your hand, and they shall be as frontlets between your eyes. You shall write them on the doorposts of your house and on your gates.

—Deuteronomy 6:6–9

- How does this passage war against the idea that a Christian need have only a superficial knowledge of Scripture?

During the Video

Answer the following questions while you watch the video. They will guide you through the lecture.

Difficulties in Approaching the Bible *0:00–12:45*

- What are two reasons given by people that explain the lack of Bible literacy in our culture?
- According to Dr. Sproul, what books of the Bible are particularly difficult for new readers of the Bible?

The Bible's Clarity and Our Calling *12:45–27:15*

- What does the *perspicuity* of Scripture mean?
- What are the two reasons we are to study the Bible?

After the Video

Answer the following questions after you have finished the lecture. They will help you identify and summarize the major points.

- Thinking critically, how do the two reasons people do not read the Bible relate to each other?

  If you are in a group, have the members identify and discuss times in their lives when they struggled with these challenges to studying the Bible. Ask them which challenge they identify with the most.

- How does the perspicuity of Scripture answer the objection that the Bible is too difficult to study and understand?

  If you are in a group, have the members work together to summarize the Bible's central message of salvation, about which the Bible is absolutely clear.

- Throughout this lesson, Dr. Sproul outlined the goals of this teaching series. How will these goals answer the two great difficulties of studying and interpreting the Bible?

  If you are in a group, have the members discuss the two reasons Dr. Sproul provided for why we are to study Scripture. Invite them to respond to the following question: How do duty and privilege relate to each other?

PRAYER

Commit what you have learned from God's Word in this lesson to prayer.

- Praise God for revealing Himself in the Bible.
- Confess ways that you fail to approach the study of the Bible as a duty and privilege.
- Thank God for the clarity of the Bible's central message of salvation in Jesus Christ.
- Ask God to make you more obedient to Him in the study of His Word by the Holy Spirit.

REVIEW QUIZ

Use these multiple-choice questions to measure what you learned from this lesson.

1. What is the perspicuity of Scripture synonymous with?
   a. Scripture's brevity
   b. Scripture's relevance
   c. Scripture's clarity
   d. Scripture's complexity

2. What challenge is raised by the claim that Scripture is a prescientific book unable to speak to the realities of modern life?
   a. Scripture is too difficult.
   b. Scripture is unclear.
   c. Scripture is irrelevant.
   d. Scripture is uninteresting.
3. What Reformer did Dr. Sproul name in connection with Scripture's perspicuity?
   a. John Knox
   b. Martin Luther
   c. John Calvin
   d. Huldrych Zwingli
4. What passage of Scripture did Dr. Sproul use to demonstrate that studying the Bible is a Christian's duty?
   a. Deuteronomy 6:4–9
   b. Psalm 119
   c. Romans 15:4
   d. 2 Timothy 3:16
5. The Gallup poll that was cited in this lesson maintained that people have a high regard for the authority of Scripture.
   a. True
   b. False
6. What two adjectives did Dr. Sproul say are actually not an insult against Scripture?
   a. Irrelevant and difficult
   b. Unauthoritative and errant
   c. Speculative and fallible
   d. Primitive and obscene

Answer Key—Why Study the Bible?

REFLECTION & DISCUSSION QUESTIONS

Before the Video

What Do You Think?

These are personal questions. The answers should be based on your own knowledge and experience.

Scripture Reading

- How does this passage war against the idea that a Christian need have only a superficial knowledge of Scripture?
  This passage reveals that God commanded Israel to dwell on His words continually. Not only are they to be on our minds, but they are to be on our hearts. These words are to be the substance of our conversations with others as we teach them about God, and they are to surround us throughout the day. God's command concerning His Word is thorough and comprehensive. Obeying will lead us beyond superficial knowledge of it.

During the Video

Difficulties in Approaching the Bible

- What are two reasons given by people that explain the lack of Bible literacy in our culture?

  The two common reasons that explain the lack of Bible literacy in our culture are that the Bible is no longer relevant to our culture and that the Bible is too difficult. The belief that the Bible is no longer relevant and that it is too difficult to interpret will be answered throughout this series by showing how correct, biblical interpretation is possible and how the principles of the Bible can be applied today. Answering these objections is at the heart of the goals for this series.

- According to Dr. Sproul, what books of the Bible are particularly difficult for new readers of the Bible?

  Many people commit to reading the Bible for the first time or start a plan to read through the Bible in a year by starting in the Old Testament in the book of Genesis. By the time the average reader has finished the book of Exodus, the laws and sanctions of the books of Leviticus, Numbers, and Deuteronomy create a seemingly insurmountable challenge. Even if a reader perseveres through these books, sorting through the kings of Judah and Israel in 1–2 Kings and 1–2 Chronicles is complex.

The Bible's Clarity and Our Calling

- What does the *perspicuity* of Scripture mean?
  One of the most important principles of the Protestant Reformation is the principle of the perspicuity of Scripture. Scripture's perspicuity refers to Scripture's clarity. When the Reformers said that Scripture is clear, they had in mind the clarity of Scripture's basic and essential message of salvation in Jesus Christ.

- What are the two reasons we are to study the Bible?

  The first reason we are to study the Bible is that it is our duty as Christians. God requires His people to be diligent students of His Word. The second reason is that studying the Bible is our privilege. In the Bible, we come to the words of life.

After the Video

- Thinking critically, how do the two reasons people do not read the Bible relate to each other?

  The two objections commonly raised to explain why people do not study the Bible relate to the Bible's relevance and the Bible's difficulty. When people object that the Bible is irrelevant, their objection often is that it, a prescientific book, cannot be applied to modern life. When people object that the Bible is too difficult, it usually relates to how far removed the history and laws of Israel are to our present experience, providing the reason they are difficult to read and understand. Both these objections relate because they appeal to the temporal and cultural distance between us and the Bible. Other logical connections between these two difficulties may also be valid.

- How does the perspicuity of Scripture answer the objection that the Bible is too difficult to study and understand?

  The perspicuity of Scripture does not mean that every part of the Bible is equally clear. Scripture's perspicuity concerns the clarity of its central message of salvation through Jesus Christ. For this reason, the perspicuity of Scripture challenges the idea that the Bible is too difficult to study and understand. Because Scripture's essential message is clear, there is eternal significance for everyone who endeavors to study it, so the difficulty of Scripture should not be a hurdle standing in the way of our study.

- Throughout this lesson, Dr. Sproul outlined the goals of this teaching series. How will these goals answer the two great difficulties of studying and interpreting the Bible?

  The primary goal of this course is to increase a person's ability and skill in interpreting the Bible. Reaching this goal will provide the key tools necessary to translate biblical principles to the present day, demonstrating how the Bible is relevant to our day. Increasing people's skill in interpretation will also help them become comfortable and confident with Scripture, alleviating its difficulty.

REVIEW QUIZ

Lesson 1

1. **C.**
The perspicuity of Scripture refers to Scripture's clarity. While the perspicuity of Scripture does not mean that every part of Scripture is equally clear, it does mean that the central message of salvation contained in Scripture is understandable through the due use of ordinary means.

2. **C.**
One of the challenges raised against studying Scripture is that Scripture is irrelevant. The Bible is often looked at as an archaic book filled with prescientific notions and an outdated moral code that doesn't speak to modern life. One of the goals of this teaching series is to demonstrate that with the proper interpretive principles, such a claim is unfounded.

3. **B.**
Scripture's perspicuity is a Protestant principle maintained by the Reformers that states an important attribute of Scripture: Scripture is clear. In this lesson, Dr. Sproul named one Reformer in relation to this attribute of Scripture: Martin Luther. Luther emphasized that the basic message of salvation is plainly revealed in Scripture.

4. **A.**
While all these passages offer wisdom into the nature of Scripture, Dr. Sproul appealed to Deuteronomy 6:4–9 to support the case that studying the Bible is a duty. This portion of Scripture contained the Shema *and calls God's people to have His words on their hearts.*

5. **A.**
Though a respect for Scripture's authority may be called into question more and more, the Gallup poll cited in this lesson indicated that people had maintained a high regard for the authority of Scripture. The problem that accompanied this finding was that despite this respect, people largely remained ignorant of the content of Scripture.

6. **D.**
Dr. Sproul was once confronted with the belligerent claim that the things contained in Scripture are primitive and obscene. He used this as an opportunity to speak about the atonement and God's grace in revealing Himself to us. In one sense, the Bible does contain the obscene, for there is nothing more obscene than the cross of Christ, when He who knew no sin became sin through imputation. In one sense, the Bible is also primitive because God condescends to us in order to reveal Himself in an understandable way through it.

2

Private Interpretation

INTRODUCTION

The principle of private interpretation is one of the most precious legacies of the Reformation. It was operative in Luther's translation of the Bible into the German language and one of the reasons we are able to study the Bible in our own homes. Yet the principle of private interpretation, on its own, can be dangerous and must be rightly understood. In this lesson, Dr. Sproul will make the proper distinctions necessary to help us understand the history and responsible practice of private interpretation.

LEARNING GOALS

When you have finished this lesson, you should be able to:

- Sketch the historical events of the Reformation relative to the practice of private interpretation
- Name and support the first principle of biblical interpretation
- Understand the dangers and obligations of private interpretation

KEY IDEAS

- Protestants are not in disagreement with the warnings of the Roman Catholic Church against subjective, private interpretation.
- There is only one correct meaning of any biblical text, though it may give rise to a multitude of applications.
- The right of private interpretation carries with it the responsibility of correct interpretation.

REFLECTION & DISCUSSION QUESTIONS

Before the Video

What Do You Think?

Take a moment to answer the following questions. They will prepare you for the lecture.

- Has anyone ever confronted you with the statement "That's your interpretation" when talking about the Bible and the significance of a passage?

- To what degree should a person's subjective experience be considered when interpreting the Bible's meaning or application?

Scripture Reading

The law of the LORD is perfect, reviving the soul; the testimony of the LORD is sure, making wise the simple; the precepts of the LORD are right, rejoicing the heart; the commandment of the LORD is pure, enlightening the eyes; the fear of the LORD is clean, enduring forever; the rules of the LORD are true, and righteous altogether.

—Psalm 19:7–9

- What adjectives are used to describe the things of God contained in Scripture?

During the Video

Answer the following questions while you watch the video. They will guide you through the lecture.

The Dangers and History of Private Interpretation *0:00–10:47*

- How did the Roman Catholic Church respond to translation of the Bible into the common vernacular?

- Why was the Roman Catholic Church opposed to vernacular translations of the Bible?

The Responsibility of Private Interpretation *10:47–27:40*

- What is the first principle of biblical interpretation?

- What working principle supports the first principle of biblical interpretation?

- What does the right of private interpretation carry along with it?

After the Video

Answer the following questions after you have finished the lecture. They will help you identify and summarize the major points.

- Martin Luther acknowledged the dangers that would accompany private interpretation. Why, then, did he persist in making a Bible translation in the vernacular of the people?

  If you are in a group, have the members discuss whether the Roman Catholic Church's resistance to private interpretation was warranted. Ask them to name any historical events that might support their claims.
- What is the primary challenge to the first principle of biblical interpretation that a Scripture passage has only one correct meaning?

  If you are in a group, have the members react to the statement "Contradiction is a hallmark of truth."
- The privilege of private interpretation comes with the responsibility of correct interpretation. What resources are available to help us correctly interpret the Bible?

  If you are in a group, have the members discuss how the responsibility that comes with private interpretation will shape their reading and studying of the Bible.

PRAYER

Commit what you have learned from God's Word in this lesson to prayer.

- Praise God as the foundation of unchanging truth.
- Confess times when you have approached God's Word irresponsibly.
- Thank God for the privilege and the responsibility of private interpretation.
- Ask God to make His Word available to those who do not have access to it.

REVIEW QUIZ

Use these multiple-choice questions to measure what you learned from this lesson.

1. What is the first principle of biblical interpretation?
   a. The meaning of Scripture's central message is clear.
   b. The Bible must be interpreted subjectively to be relevant.
   c. There is only one correct meaning of any biblical text.
   d. The Bible should be studied privately and responsibly.

2. What responsibility comes along with the right of private interpretation?
   a. Subjective interpretation
   b. Infallible interpretation
   c. Correct interpretation
   d. Literal interpretation

3. What did one twentieth-century theologian call the "hallmark of truth"?
   a. Authority
   b. Necessity
   c. Validation
   d. Contradiction

4. What was *not* a reason why the Roman Catholic Church reacted against vernacular translations of the Bible?
   a. It feared that vernacular translations would lead to private interpretation.
   b. It feared that the church would be exposed for departing from biblical truth.
   c. It feared that people would erroneously interpret the doctrines of the Bible.
   d. It feared the proliferation of different Christian denominations.

5. The principle of private interpretation establishes subjective interpretation.
   a. True
   b. False

6. What is the process that reads an outside meaning into a biblical text called?
   a. Exegesis
   b. Eisegesis
   c. Synegesis
   d. Prosegesis

Answer Key—Private Interpretation

REFLECTION & DISCUSSION QUESTIONS

Before the Video

What Do You Think?

These are personal questions. The answers should be based on your own knowledge and experience.

Scripture Reading

- What adjectives are used to describe the things of God contained in Scripture? *Four different words are used in this passage to name the things of God contained in Scripture: God's "law," "precepts," "commandment," and "rules." The adjectives used to describe these are "perfect," "right," "pure," and "true." Furthermore, the fear of God, a desired result of studying Scripture, is called "clean." All these adjectives should inform how we interpret and approach God's Word.*

During the Video

The Dangers and History of Private Interpretation

- How did the Roman Catholic Church respond to translation of the Bible into the common vernacular?

  Martyrdom was often the cost for the initial translations of the Bible into the common vernacular of the people. Though Luther did not face death for his efforts to translate the Bible into German, the Roman Catholic Church did attempt to suppress the publication of the Bible in other languages.

- Why was the Roman Catholic Church opposed to vernacular translations of the Bible?

  The Roman Catholic Church opposed vernacular translations because it feared that people would be led into erroneous understandings of Scripture to the damnation of their souls. It also feared that different interpretations of the Bible would lead to different church denominations and that the church would then be fragmented and fractured.

The Responsibility of Private Interpretation

- What is the first principle of biblical interpretation?

  The first principle of biblical interpretation is that there is only one correct meaning of any biblical text. Though there is only one correct meaning of any biblical text, there may be various applications and multiple layers of significance within a text.

- What working principle supports the first principle of biblical interpretation?

  The working principle that supports the truth that any biblical text has only one correct meaning is that the truth is not contradictory. The Word of God is truth and, as truth, is consistent in every way. For this reason, having contradictory interpretations of a single passage implies that all those interpretations except one must be wrong.

- What does the right of private interpretation carry along with it?

  The right of private interpretation carries with it the responsibility of correct interpretation. Handling the Word of God is a significant responsibility, and we must not become guilty of the kind of private interpretation that makes the Bible say whatever we want.

After the Video

- Martin Luther acknowledged the dangers that would accompany private interpretation. Why, then, did he persist in making a Bible translation in the vernacular of the people?

  Martin Luther did not disagree with the Roman Catholic Church's fears regarding private interpretation that the Bible would be wrongly interpreted. Nevertheless, Luther persisted in translating the Bible into the vernacular because of his foundational belief in the clarity of Scripture's central message and the conviction that the gospel of Jesus Christ was not being preached and was therefore desperately needed.

- What is the primary challenge to the first principle of biblical interpretation that a Scripture passage has only one correct meaning?

  The primary challenge to the first principle of biblical interpretation is the rejection of the principle in favor of a subjective or relativistic approach to interpreting Scripture. Such an approach to Scripture collapses the Bible's authority as the Word of God and makes way for deficient views that truth itself can be contradictory.

- The privilege of private interpretation comes with the responsibility of correct interpretation. What resources are available to help us correctly interpret the Bible?

  Because the responsibility of correct interpretation accompanies our privilege of private interpretation, we must strive to use the best resources and interpretive principles when studying the Bible. Some of the resources available to help us interpret the Bible correctly are the historic creeds and confessions of the church, commentaries, and the other works of theologians today and throughout church history.

REVIEW QUIZ

Lesson 2

1. **C.**
The first principle of biblical interpretation is that any biblical text has only one correct meaning. This principle of interpretation must be applied during private study and overrides subjective interpretations about the truth claims of Scripture.

2. **C.**
The right of private interpretation carries along with it the weighty task of correctly interpreting the Bible as God's Word. Knowing that we are not infallible, we must undertake this task with humility and the willingness to study diligently, seeking needed guidance.

3. **D.**
The twentieth-century theologian Emil Brunner said, "Contradiction is the hallmark of truth." In this lesson, Dr. Sproul used this quote to show how such a belief undermines objective truth, making contradiction, in fact, the hallmark of falsehood.

4. **B.**
The Roman Catholic Church was not trying to hide its departure from biblical truth in suppressing new translations of the Bible. Although this suppression seems nefarious on the surface, the Roman Catholic Church had genuine concern for souls.

5. **B.**
If the meaning of a Bible passage were a matter of subjective interpretation, then the authority of Scripture would collapse. The first principle of biblical interpretation is that any passage has only one correct meaning. Yet the application of a passage does speak to individual, subjective experience.

6. **B.**
The word eisegesis *contains the Greek preposition* eis, *which means "into." Eisegesis, unlike exegesis, reads meaning into a text as opposed to reading it from the text. Eisegesis reads something into a text that isn't there, and so it draws an interpretation out of it illegitimately.*

3

The Science of Interpretation

INTRODUCTION

Everyone who reads the Bible is engaged in a method of understanding the Bible. The question now is whether the method of interpretation you use really reveals the truth of God as intended by the Holy Spirit. In this lesson, Dr. Sproul surveys modern crises of biblical interpretation and defines three competing approaches to it.

LEARNING GOALS

When you have finished this lesson, you should be able to:

- Understand the influence of nineteenth-century liberalism on the interpretation of the Bible
- Name and define three methods of biblical interpretation and their implications

KEY IDEAS

- There is a subdivision of theology exclusively concerned with the principles that ought to govern our interpretation of Scripture.
- Nineteenth-century liberal theology demythologized the Bible, while attempting to maintain its moral relevance to modern life.
- The classical orthodox Protestant approach of biblical interpretation is the grammatico-historical method.

REFLECTION & DISCUSSION QUESTIONS

Before the Video

What Do You Think?

Take a moment to answer the following questions. They will prepare you for the lecture.

- What are the central doctrines of the Christian faith?

- How important is your historical setting to interpreting Scripture?

Scripture Reading

Concerning this salvation, the prophets who prophesied about the grace that was to be yours searched and inquired carefully, inquiring what person or time the Spirit of Christ in them was indicating when he predicted the sufferings of Christ and the subsequent glories. It was revealed to them that they were serving not themselves but you, in the things that have now been announced to you through those who preached the good news to you by the Holy Spirit sent from heaven, things into which angels long to look.

—1 Peter 1:10–12

- What does this passage reveal about the modern relevance of Scripture?

During the Video

Answer the following questions while you watch the video. They will guide you through the lecture.

Interpretation as Art and Science *0:00–15:06*

- What rule of interpretation emerged in modern art?

- What are the two dimensions to the principle that any Scripture passage has only one correct meaning?

- What is the subdivision of theology that deals with the principles of interpretation called?

Methods of Interpretation *15:06–29:40*

- What is the classical Protestant approach to interpretation? What is its aim?

- What approach to interpretation was influenced by the theory of evolution? What did it state?

- What approach to interpretation emphasizes our personal experience of Scripture? According to that approach, how do we experience the Word of God?

After the Video

Answer the following questions after you have finished the lecture. They will help you identify and summarize the major points.

- How would you describe nineteenth-century liberalism? What did it seek to eliminate from the Bible? What did it seek to maintain?

  If you are in a group, have the members discuss whether nineteenth-century liberal theology is consistent in its hermeneutic of Scripture.

- How do the religious-historical and the existential approaches to interpretation conflict with the grammatico-historical method?

  If you are in a group, have the members discuss whether the religious-historical and the existential approaches to interpretation offer any helpful insights about how to interact with the Bible.

- What would happen if the religious-historical or existential method prevailed over the grammatico-historical method of interpretation?

  If you are in a group, have the members discuss which three approaches to interpretation exert the most influence on today's evangelicals and why.

PRAYER

Commit what you have learned from God's Word in this lesson to prayer.

- Praise God for His supreme authority as the Author of all truth.
- Confess any times you've prioritized your experience over Scripture.
- Thank God for preserving His Word in writing so that you can study it.
- Ask God for the assistance of the Holy Spirit as you study the Bible.

REVIEW QUIZ

Use these multiple-choice questions to measure what you learned from this lesson.

1. What word best describes the nature of the meaning of Scripture?
    a. Abstract
    b. Subjective
    c. Objective
    d. Arcane
2. What is the science of biblical interpretation called?
    a. Apologetics
    b. Hermeneutics
    c. Hamartiology
    d. Homiletics
3. What elements of the Bible did nineteenth-century liberalism want to eliminate?
    a. Moral
    b. Historical
    c. Supernatural
    d. Theological
4. What influenced the religious-historical method of interpretation?
    a. Evolution
    b. Feminism
    c. Liberalism
    d. Victorianism
5. The grammatico-historical method does not deal with modern-day application.
    a. True
    b. False
6. What method of interpretation most closely aligns with the analogy that interpreting the Bible is like interpreting modern art?
    a. Grammatico-historical
    b. Religious-historical
    c. Existential
    d. Exegetical

Answer Key—The Science of Interpretation

REFLECTION & DISCUSSION QUESTIONS

Before the Video

What Do You Think?

These are personal questions. The answers should be based on your own knowledge and experience.

Scripture Reading

- What does this passage reveal about the modern relevance of Scripture?

  This passage reveals that even the prophets of the Old Testament were aware that they were serving future generations in their prophecies about the sufferings and glory of Christ. The Apostles were aware of this reality in their own writings as well. This helps us understand how Scripture's relevance extends beyond its immediate audience and even to us who partake of the grace of Jesus Christ today, which means that it is applicable not just to our salvation but to all our lives.

During the Video

Interpretation as Art and Science

- What rule of interpretation emerged in modern art?

  The new rule in certain art movements stated that the meaning of an artwork is no longer determined by the artist; it is determined by the observer. This was a conscious step to embrace a subjectivism devoid of objective meaning.

- What are the two dimensions to the principle that any Scripture passage has only one correct meaning?

  The objective meaning of Scripture can be approached from two levels: the level of the human author's intention and the level of the divine author's intention. Ultimately, Scripture is a revelation of God through the agency of the Holy Spirit, so the authorial intention of Scripture is unified, and meaning is objectively determined by its author.

- What is the subdivision of theology that deals with the principles of interpretation called?

  The subdivision of theology that deals with the principles of interpretation is called hermeneutics, *deriving from the Greek meaning "to interpret."*

Methods of Interpretation

- What is the classical Protestant approach to interpretation? What is its aim?

  The classical Protestant approach to interpretation is the grammatico-historical method, which strives to discover the original meaning of the text through grammatical, lexical, syntactical, and historical considerations, while applying it to the modern day.

- What approach to interpretation was influenced by the theory of evolution? What did it state?

  The method of interpretation that was influenced by Darwin's theory of evolution and subsequent social theories of the nineteenth century is the religious-historical method. It stated that religion evolves from simple to complex, mutating from primitive forms of animism and polytheism and eventually reaching monotheism.

- What approach to interpretation emphasizes our personal experience of Scripture? According to that approach, how do we experience the Word of God?

  The method of interpretation that emphasizes personal experience is the existential method. The existential method was born out of the perceived need for theology to be timeless, not bound to its immediate audience or even to the present day. The Bible then transcends time and is experienced directly from God, and only in that existential experience does it become the Word of God to us.

After the Video

- How would you describe nineteenth-century liberalism? What did it seek to eliminate from the Bible? What did it seek to maintain?

  Nineteenth-century liberalism was a reaction to the modern, industrialized, scientific world. This movement believed that the Bible was not compatible with these developments, which resulted in a crisis of belief. In order to alleviate this crisis, theologians of this school attempted to demythologize Scripture, dismissing every supernatural event in the Bible. By doing this, they were still able to appeal to the moral teachings of Jesus Christ as a solution to the world's ethical and social problems.

- How do the religious-historical and the existential approaches to interpretation conflict with the grammatico-historical method?

  The religious-historical method conflicts with the grammatico-historical method by imposing the concept of an evolution of religious thought onto the text of Scripture, making the Old Testament a primitive stage of historical development. The existential method conflicts with the grammatico-historical method by denying the objectivity of the Word of God and its historical nature, allowing for the Bible to become the Word of God only when it meets us in our existential experience. The grammatico-historical method upholds the authority of the authors of Scripture.

- What would happen if the religious-historical or existential method prevailed over the grammatico-historical method of interpretation?

  Dr. Sproul ended this lesson by saying, "If the new hermeneutic prevails, then we will have a Jesus who is not the same yesterday, today, and forever." The objectivity of the Bible would be destroyed, and its very witness about the nature of God and the person and work of Jesus Christ could be called into question if we asserted ourselves over Scripture instead of humbly coming under it.

REVIEW QUIZ

Lesson 3

1. **C.**
   The perspicuity of Scripture works against the idea that the meaning of Scripture is arcane or abstract in nature. Scripture also cannot be purely subjective, though there is a subjective aspect to applying Scripture to our situations. Rather, Scripture's meaning is always objective, pointing back to the reality that God is its Author.

2. **B.**
   Apologetics is the defense of the Christian faith. Hamartiology is a division of systematic theology that focuses on sin. Homiletics is the study of preaching. Hermeneutics is the area of study that deals with biblical interpretation.

3. **C.**
   Nineteenth-century liberalism is odd in that it tried to maintain the moral teachings of Jesus Christ while dismissing His supernatural works and all other supernatural events that occurred in Scripture. In one sense, this attacks the historical and theological elements of the Bible, but nineteenth-century liberalism was primarily reacting to a crisis of faith due to the perceived incompatibility of the Bible with the modern world.

4. **A.**
   The religious-historical method of interpretation was significantly influenced by the theory of evolution and the impact of that theory on philosophical, economic, and social arenas. It asserted that religions all evolve from simple to complex, from animism all the way to monotheism.

5. **B.**
   While the grammatico-historical hermeneutic seeks to uphold the historical meaning of the text, it also seeks to bridge the gap between ancient history and the twenty-first century in order to apply Scripture today. The grammatico-historical method resists the temptation of allowing our own experience to interpret the authorial intent in Scripture.

6. **C.**
   In the beginning of this lesson, Dr. Sproul surveyed a trend in modern art to give the observer the power to interpret the meaning of an artwork, apart from any intended meaning of the artist. The method of interpretation that is analogous to this is the existential method, because through it the Bible is subjected to our experience.

4

Literal Interpretation

INTRODUCTION

The Bible is more than an ancient book of ethical instructions. It's nothing less than the Word of God. But how should we read and understand it? Should we read it literally? In this lesson, Dr. Sproul explains that the only way to interpret the Bible is through a literal interpretation, and then he looks at what this approach means.

LEARNING GOALS

When you have finished this lesson, you should be able to:

- Explain the meaning and function of the literal interpretation of the Bible
- Understand how both liberal and conservative Christians tend to distort the meaning of the Bible through the way they approach it
- Define the *sensus literalis* of Scripture

KEY IDEAS

- What it means to interpret the Bible literally is often misunderstood.
- Rightly understanding what it means to interpret the Bible literally protects someone from dangerous, spiritualistic methods of interpretation.
- The Bible should be interpreted according to its literary forms.
- Questions about whether to believe the Bible should come after the interpretation of its meaning.

REFLECTION & DISCUSSION QUESTIONS

Before the Video

What Do You Think?

Take a moment to answer the following questions. They will prepare you for the lecture.

- What does it mean to interpret the Bible literally?

- Have you ever randomly opened the Bible for an answer to a dilemma or for a passage to study? Would you defend such a practice?

Scripture Reading

But he, desiring to justify himself, said to Jesus, "And who is my neighbor?" Jesus replied, "A man was going down from Jerusalem to Jericho, and he fell among robbers, who stripped him and beat him and departed, leaving him half dead. Now by chance a priest was going down that road, and when he saw him he passed by on the other side. So likewise a Levite, when he came to the place and saw him, passed by on the other side. But a Samaritan, as he journeyed, came to where he was, and when he saw him, he had compassion. He went to him and bound up his wounds, pouring on oil and wine. Then he set him on his own animal and brought him to an inn and took care of him. And the next day he took out two denarii and gave them to the innkeeper, saying, 'Take care of him, and whatever more you spend, I will repay you when I come back.' Which of these three, do you think, proved to be a neighbor to the man who fell among the robbers?" He said, "The one who showed him mercy." And Jesus said to him, "You go, and do likewise."

—Luke 10:29–37

- What important features of this passage help you to know how to interpret it?

During the Video

Answer the following questions while you watch the video. They will guide you through the lecture.

The Meaning of Literal Interpretation *0:00–13:40*

- What is usually assumed about the literal interpretation of the Bible?

- What is the *sensus literalis* of Scripture?

- What is the literal interpretation of Scripture opposed to? What does this other method turn the Bible into?

The Challenges of Literal Interpretation *13:40–28:08*

- What does a literal interpretation of the Bible first require us to recognize?

- What needs to come after the interpretation of the meaning of Scripture? Why?

After the Video

Answer the following questions after you have finished the lecture. They will help you identify and summarize the major points.

- Should we interpret the Bible like any other book? If so, in what sense?

  If you are in a group, have the members discuss their experience with the spiritualistic approach to the Bible. Ask them whether this approach seems responsible given that the Bible uses common literary conventions.

- What is the difference between the experiences of Augustine and Jonathan Edwards and those of Dr. Sproul's friends?

  If you are in a group, have the members read the passages of Scripture that Augustine (Rom. 13:13–14) and Edwards (1 Tim. 1:17) encountered. Ask the group members how the literal interpretation of these passages addressed the situations of these men.

- How might liberal and conservative Christians be guilty of reinterpreting Scripture?

  If you are in a group, have the members scan through the book of Jonah. Invite them to respond to the following questions: What literary features of the book of Jonah make it difficult to evaluate in terms of genre? What events would cause problems for a theological liberal? What points to the book's historicity?

PRAYER

Commit what you have learned from God's Word in this lesson to prayer.

- Praise God for the literary richness of expression found in Scripture.
- Confess ways that you have irresponsibly approached the Bible.
- Thank God for His promise to use His Word for your sanctification.
- Ask God to guard you from becoming puffed up in knowledge.

REVIEW QUIZ

Use these multiple-choice questions to measure what you learned from this lesson.

1. What Latin phrase was used for the key interpretive principle of this lesson?
   a. *Sensus divinitatis*
   b. *Sola Scriptura*
   c. *Sensus literalis*
   d. *Analogia fide*
2. Literal interpretation looks for the plain sense of a passage without the need for considering its literary form.
   a. True
   b. False
3. What word was used in this lesson to describe the type of interpretation we need?
   a. Charitable
   b. Prophetic
   c. Godly
   d. Sober
4. Dr. Sproul argued that the book of Jonah primarily takes what literary form?
   a. Poetic
   b. Historical
   c. Didactic
   d. Apocalyptic
5. Since the Bible is the Word of God, we dare not interpret it like any other book.
   a. True
   b. False
6. Who experienced a dramatic transformation to the Christian faith when he overheard the refrain "Take up and read!" and picked up a Bible?
   a. Augustine
   b. Jonathan Edwards
   c. Martin Luther
   d. John Calvin

Answer Key—Literal Interpretation

REFLECTION & DISCUSSION QUESTIONS

Before the Video

What Do You Think?

These are personal questions. The answers should be based on your own knowledge and experience.

Scripture Reading

- What important features of this passage help you to know how to interpret it?

  This passage contains the parable of the good Samaritan. The fact that this teaching from Jesus is a parable helps us know how to interpret it. Because it is a parable, we do not need to ask questions about whether the men in the parable existed. It is intended to teach something—namely, that the man who desired to know who his neighbor was should show mercy to those he least expected. Because this parable is rooted in the relationship that existed between Jews and Samaritans, there are important historical features to be considered for a correct, literal interpretation.

During the Video

The Meaning of Literal Interpretation

- What is usually assumed about the literal interpretation of the Bible?

  It is often assumed that the literal interpretation of the Bible is upheld by uneducated people who have an anti-intellectual mentality. This assumption is based on a misconception of what it means to interpret the Bible literally.

- What is the *sensus literalis* of Scripture?

  The sensus literalis *of Scripture means the "literal sense" of Scripture. It is a science of interpretation rooted in the Reformation and closely related to the grammatico-historical method discussed in the previous lesson. It seeks the plain sense of Scripture by honoring the literary forms of Scripture, following normal rules of literary interpretation.*

- What is the literal interpretation of Scripture opposed to? What does this other method turn the Bible into?

  The principle of the literal interpretation of the Bible is opposed to the spiritualistic interpretation of the Bible, which looks for hidden, secret, or mysterious meaning in the Bible. A spiritualistic approach to the Bible turns the Bible into a superstitious tool of magic.

The Challenges of Literal Interpretation

- What does a literal interpretation of the Bible first require us to recognize?

  Far from being unsophisticated, a literal interpretation of the Bible requires us to be able to recognize the literary forms of Scripture. For example, we need to be able to distinguish between poetry, prophecy, historical narrative, wisdom literature, and didactic teachings.

- What needs to come after the interpretation of the meaning of Scripture? Why?

  The Word of God is truth, yet the question of belief and unbelief is one that needs to come after the interpretation of Scripture. The reason is that the presuppositions that people bring to the Bible can distort it and cause them to reinterpret its meaning.

After the Video

- Should we interpret the Bible like any other book? If so, in what sense?

  On the one hand, the Bible is the Word of God and should be approached as such. Yet the rules for interpreting the Bible are no different from the rules for interpreting any other book. The Bible is God's special revelation to us through the medium of human language, which means that the vocabulary, grammar, and syntax of a language, as well as various literary forms, ought to be studied in an ordinary way when it comes to the Bible.

- What is the difference between the experiences of Augustine and Jonathan Edwards and those of Dr. Sproul's friends?

  In the cases of Augustine and Edwards, God used the literal meaning of a passage to convict or bring about a spiritual change. In the case of Dr. Sproul's friends, they interpreted Scripture apart from its literal meaning. While the practice of blindly opening the Bible for an answer is irresponsible, the Bible must still be interpreted according to its literal meaning in accord with responsible methods of interpretation.

- How might liberal and conservative Christians be guilty of reinterpreting Scripture?

  It is paramount that the literal meaning of Scripture be maintained regardless of a person's theological framework. For theological liberals, the challenge they bring to interpreting Scripture is their unbelief in important features of Scripture such as accounts of miracles. Therefore, they reinterpret passages that contain miracles, attempting to explain them away. For theological conservatives, there may be a temptation to interpret Scripture through a crass literalism that doesn't take a passage's literary form or original meaning into account. An example of this is reading into prophecy or making the application of a passage its primary meaning.

REVIEW QUIZ

Lesson 4

1. **C.**
   The key concept of the literal interpretation of the Bible was captured by the Latin phrase sensus literalis, *which means "literal sense." Finding the literal sense of a passage involves identifying its literary form and goes beyond rigid literalism.*

2. **B.**
   A key component of the literal interpretation of Scripture is considering a passage's literary form. This is what can help us determine whether language is literal (as in the case of historical narrative) or figurative (as in the case of poetry).

3. **D.**
   Many times in this lesson, Dr. Sproul identified the type of interpretation we need with the modifier sober. *This word pushes back against mystical or spiritualistic tendencies to treat the Bible as a book of hidden meaning. Martin Luther's call in the Reformation was for a return to sober biblical interpretation.*

4. **B.**
   Dr. Sproul argued that the book of Jonah is historical narrative. Though it contains poetry, the book communicates to us historical events, and it should not be considered purely didactic or moral. It tells us something about events that actually happened.

5. **B.**
   Because God uses human language and the various conventions of language to reveal Himself to us in Scripture, it is natural to interpret the Bible as we would other books. Though our posture toward Scripture may differ from that toward an ordinary book, we must still approach the Bible in an ordinary way to determine its meaning.

6. **A.**
   Augustine heard this refrain and picked up a Bible, opening to Romans 13:13–14 and experiencing a radical shift to the Christian faith. Dr. Sproul used this as an example of a haphazard approach to the Bible but one that at least did justice to the plain sense of Scripture.

5

Literary Forms, Part 1

INTRODUCTION

Christians are called to take Scripture seriously and literally. But how exactly do we do that? If we are rigidly literalistic, then we actually do an injustice to the way that the Bible is intended to be read. Just as we must acknowledge the various genres of Scripture, we must also recognize the type of language that Scripture uses. In this lesson, Dr. Sproul presents the various literary techniques that convey the trustworthy and inerrant meaning of Scripture.

LEARNING GOALS

When you have finished this lesson, you should be able to:

- Recognize multiple literary forms that are encountered in the Bible
- Explain how understanding the language of Scripture clears up misconceptions about the Bible

KEY IDEAS

- The Bible uses a simple language of appearance and commonly uses round numbers to describe events as they appear in everyday experience.
- The Bible uses hyperbolic, metaphorical, and anthropomorphic language to communicate meaningful information in an intentional, ordinary, and understandable way.

REFLECTION & DISCUSSION QUESTIONS

Before the Video

What Do You Think?

Take a moment to answer the following questions. They will prepare you for the lecture.

- Is biblical language different from the language you encounter in other books? If so, how?

- Why does the Bible use human terms to talk about God?

Scripture Reading

But the hour is coming, and is now here, when the true worshipers will worship the Father in spirit and truth, for the Father is seeking such people to worship him. God is spirit, and those who worship him must worship in spirit and truth.

—John 4:23–24

For the wrath of God is revealed from heaven against all ungodliness and unrighteousness of men, who by their unrighteousness suppress the truth. For what can be known about God is plain to them, because God has shown it to them. For his invisible attributes, namely, his eternal power and divine nature, have been clearly perceived, ever since the creation of the world, in the things that have been made. So they are without excuse.

—Romans 1:18–20

- What do these two passages, taken together, stress about God's nature?

During the Video

Answer the following questions while you watch the video. They will guide you through the lecture.

The Language of Appearances *0:00–11:48*

- What is the technical term for the language of appearances?

- In what sense is it not incorrect to use the language of appearances?

- What way of approaching the Bible creates unnecessary problems with science?

Hyperbole, Metaphor, and Anthropomorphism *11:48–27:37*

- What key element in a definition of hyperbole makes it more than a mere exaggeration of fact?

- How does the statement "I am the vine; you are the branches" (John 15:5) illustrate the purpose of metaphorical language?

- What is the etymology of the word *anthropomorphic*?

After the Video

Answer the following questions after you have finished the lecture. They will help you identify and summarize the major points.

- What is often at the root of the issue for scientific objections to the Bible and was even on display when the church rejected the scientific findings of Galileo Galilei?

  If you are in a group, have the members come up with a list of biblical truths that have bearing on scientific claims. As an example of such a truth, Dr. Sproul discussed the reality that the world was created by God.

- Why does the Bible use anthropomorphic language?

  If you are in a group, have the members look up the following passages that use this type of language and identify what meaning is being conveyed by it: Ex. 3:20; 33:21–23; Num. 6:25; Deut. 4:34; 2 Sam. 22:7; 2 Chron. 7:16; Job 40:9; Ps. 34:15; Isa. 59:1.

- Out of the five different literary features of the Bible that were discussed in this lesson, which one have you struggled with the most in the past? What are some examples?

  If you are in a group, have the members discuss the answers and the following question: Why do people seem to hold the Bible to a different standard than they would for any other book?

PRAYER

Commit what you have learned from God's Word in this lesson to prayer.

- Praise God for His profound self-revelation in the person of His Son.
- Confess any disregard for the richness and majesty of God's Word.
- Thank God for the diversity through which He has revealed Himself.
- Ask God to make you more aware of the richness of His Word.

REVIEW QUIZ

Use these multiple-choice questions to measure what you learned from this lesson.

1. What is the intentional use of exaggeration to make a point?
   a. Merism
   b. Metaphor
   c. Hyperbole
   d. Anthropomorphism
2. What manner of speech describes God in human terms?
   a. Hyperbolic
   b. Metaphoric
   c. Anthropomorphic
   d. Phenomenological
3. The Bible typically uses mathematical precision in its description of events.
   a. True
   b. False
4. What type of language plays a role in theological differences of the Reformation over the Lord's Supper?
   a. Hyperbolic
   b. Metaphoric
   c. Anthropomorphic
   d. Phenomenological
5. The Bible should not be approached as precise scientific literature.
   a. True
   b. False
6. What is God's supreme example of anthropomorphic revelation?
   a. The special revelation of Holy Scripture
   b. The incarnation of the Son of God
   c. The general revelation in creation
   d. The human language of Scripture

Answer Key—Literary Forms, Part 1

REFLECTION & DISCUSSION QUESTIONS

Before the Video

What Do You Think?

These are personal questions. The answers should be based on your own knowledge and experience.

Scripture Reading

- What do these two passages, taken together, stress about God's nature?

  In John 4:24, Jesus clearly states, "God is spirit," and Romans 1:20 speaks of God's "invisible attributes." One important feature of these two passages is the truth that, as a spirit with invisible attributes, God does not have a body like a man.

During the Video

The Language of Appearances

- What is the technical term for the language of appearances?

  The technical term for the language of appearances is phenomenological language. *The phenomena of everyday experience are the observable facts, occurrences, or circumstances we encounter.*

- In what sense is it not incorrect to use the language of appearances?

  While phenomenological language may not be scientifically precise, describing things as they appear to the naked eye is not incorrect. This language is merely descriptive of our perceptions, and in this sense, it is not erroneous if understood as a common way of communicating perceived human experience.

- What way of approaching the Bible creates unnecessary problems with science?

  Approaching the Bible as if it were a scientific textbook that uses precise scientific language will inevitably collide with scientific discovery. We must be careful not to force the Bible into a never-intended mode of communicating truth about the world around us. This is not to say that conflict will then never arise, for the Bible makes profound claims that have profound implications for scientific questions.

Hyperbole, Metaphor, and Anthropomorphism

- What key element in a definition of hyperbole makes it more than a mere exaggeration of fact?

  Hyperbole is a literary technique that exaggerates a fact or a general truth. In one sense, hyperbole could be called a distortion of the truth, but hyperbole has a key element that distinguishes it from a mere falsehood: hyperbole is an intentional *exaggeration of facts in order to make a point. In this sense, it serves the truth as a legitimate literary technique.*

- How does the statement "I am the vine; you are the branches" (John 15:5) illustrate the purpose of metaphorical language?

  The Bible uses metaphor to illustrate truths by comparing things to objects in nature or everyday experience. Jesus did this often in His ministry. His statement "I am the vine; you are the branches" is one such instance in which a figurative analogy is being drawn. Jesus is not literally a vine, nor are His disciples branches, but the direct correlation of their abiding in Him and bearing fruit is communicated.

- What is the etymology of the word *anthropomorphic*?

  The word anthropomorphic *comes from two Greek words. The first is* anthrōpos, *which means "man," as in the word* anthropology. *The second is* morphē, *which means "form," as in the word* metamorphosis.

After the Video

- What is often at the root of the issue for scientific objections to the Bible and was even on display when the church rejected the scientific findings of Galileo Galilei?

  The real conflict at certain points between science and biblical truth claims is often over a misunderstanding of either the claims of science or the claims of Scripture. An example from a scientific perspective is someone's taking issue with Scripture for using phenomenological language. The church itself was guilty of this misunderstanding in Galileo's case: this language of Scripture was not identified, and the issue of geocentricism became a matter of church dogma.

- Why does the Bible use anthropomorphic language?

  The Bible uses anthropomorphic language so that we might understand truth about who God is. As human beings, we are made in the image of God, so there is a point of contact that makes it possible to speak truthfully about God by means of analogy. Through His Word, God takes the initiative to speak to us, and He does so in human terms, in ways that we understand, because we have finite minds. To reveal Himself, God condescends to our weakness, something that He did most profoundly through the incarnation of the Son.

- Out of the five different literary features of the Bible that were discussed in this lesson, which one have you struggled with the most in the past? What are some examples?

  This is a personal question, so answers will vary, but they should focus on the phenomenological language, round numbers, hyperbole, metaphor, and anthropomorphisms of the Bible.

REVIEW QUIZ

Lesson 5

1. **C.**
Hyperbole is a way of intentionally making a point through the use of exaggeration. While some may argue that this is a distortion of the truth, the use of hyperbole is common and is generally understood to be an exaggeration of something truthful.

2. **C.**
Language that is anthropomorphic, from the Greek words meaning "man" and "form," is employed in the Bible in order to communicate truth about God by way of analogy. This analogy is possible because man is created in God's image.

3. **B.**
Closely related to the use of phenomenological language, rounded numerical totals are often presented in the Bible. This rounding is related to the language of appearance because the number of people in a group would have been calculated according to the perception of the naked eye.

4. **B.**
In Matthew 26:26, Jesus said to His disciples, "Take, eat; this is my body." Jesus was speaking either literally or figuratively, and this question was significant for the Reformers' treatment of the Lord's Supper. Martin Luther did not allow for the possibility that Jesus was using metaphorical language, whereas John Calvin did.

5. **A.**
The various literary forms found in Scripture and discussed in this lesson argue against approaching Scripture as if it were a science textbook. This approach leads only to more conflict with science because the Bible is not taken on its own terms. Yet many truths in the Bible have profound bearing on scientific inquiry.

6. **B.**
Anthropomorphism is a common figure of speech found in Scripture because it is a means by which God can communicate to us something truthful about Himself. The most supreme form of this, however, is the Son of God's becoming flesh in the incarnation.

6

Literary Forms, Part 2

INTRODUCTION

Many biblical accounts and narratives are written off as fable or myth against antisupernatural presuppositions. How do we understand these stories in light of redemptive history? How can we tell the difference between fable and history? In this lesson, Dr. Sproul explains the fundamental differences between the two as he continues to expand on the various literary forms found in Scripture.

LEARNING GOALS

When you have finished this lesson, you should be able to:

- Define the elements of personification and historical narrative
- Identify passages that present challenges to literary classification

KEY IDEAS

- Personification is a poetic device used frequently in Scripture to describe inanimate objects.
- Some biblical passages are difficult to isolate into and identify as one literary category.
- The question about the Bible's historicity is one about the Bible's trustworthiness as redemptive *history*.
- A key to reading Scripture on its own terms is being able to identify historical narrative.

REFLECTION & DISCUSSION QUESTIONS

Before the Video

What Do You Think?

Take a moment to answer the following questions. They will prepare you for the lecture.

- Why do you believe in a historical fall and a historical Adam and Eve?

- What other historical accounts in Scripture could be called into question if events such as the fall were questioned?

Scripture Reading

In those days a decree went out from Caesar Augustus that all the world should be registered. This was the first registration when Quirinius was governor of Syria. And all went to be registered, each to his own town. And Joseph also went up from Galilee, from the town of Nazareth, to Judea, to the city of David, which is called Bethlehem, because he was of the house and lineage of David, to be registered with Mary, his betrothed, who was with child.

—Luke 2:1–5

- What elements in this passage indicate that it is written as historical narrative?

During the Video

Answer the following questions while you watch the video. They will guide you through the lecture.

Personification *0:00–19:12*

- What is personification?

- What are two passages where the line seems blurred between historical narrative and the personification that is commonly found in poetry?

- What crisis is related to questions about the presence of personification in historical narratives?

Historical Narrative *19:12–27:30*

- What are some of the normal features of historical narrative?

- Who bears the burden of proof when different literary forms are present in historical narrative and a passage's historicity is questioned?

After the Video

Answer the following questions after you have finished the lecture. They will help you identify and summarize the major points.

- What natural conclusion follows from rejection of a talking serpent in Genesis 3 as historically unbelievable?

  If you are in a group, have the members read Genesis 2:4; 5:1; 6:9; 10:1; 11:27; 25:12, 19; 36:1; 37:2. Ask the group what clues in the text help to make a case for the historicity of the early chapters of Genesis.

- What might be the problem of the person who is skeptical that the account of the fall is historical? How would you try to convince the person otherwise?

  If you are in a group, have the members read Genesis 2–3 and ask them to identify the historical elements and different literary forms.

- Why is it critical that we defend the historicity of the Bible?

  If you are in a group, have the members discuss openly any passages in the Bible that have challenged them. Have them share the truths about God or doctrines of the faith that have helped resolve or ease the tension of those challenges.

PRAYER

Commit what you have learned from God's Word in this lesson to prayer.

- Praise God for His display of sovereign power over creation and history.
- Confess any doubts you have about the accurate historical nature of the Bible.
- Thank God for the illuminating work of the Holy Spirit that you've experienced.
- Ask God to continue to make Scripture plain to you in your studies.

REVIEW QUIZ

Use these multiple-choice questions to measure what you learned from this lesson.

1. What literary form most commonly features personification?
   a. Poetry
   b. Epistle
   c. Parable
   d. Historical narrative

2. Denying its status as historical narrative, how do some commentators label the story of Balaam's donkey?
   a. Parable
   b. Poetry
   c. Fable
   d. Satire

3. "Did the snake speak?" How did Karl Barth respond to this question?
   a. By denying the Bible's historicity
   b. By affirming the historical claims of Genesis 3
   c. By rephrasing the question to focus on the content of the serpent's speech
   d. By conceding that the question was critical to Scripture's redemptive claims

4. What is *not* a clear feature of historical narrative?
   a. Prose style
   b. Genealogies
   c. Moral lessons
   d. Geographical location

5. The early chapters of Genesis have plain historical features.
   a. True
   b. False

6. What literary genre is at the center of controversy over the Christian faith?
   a. Hebrew poetry
   b. Wisdom literature
   c. Historical narrative
   d. Apocalyptic literature

Answer Key— Literary Forms, Part 2

REFLECTION & DISCUSSION QUESTIONS

Before the Video

What Do You Think?

These are personal questions. The answers should be based on your own knowledge and experience.

Scripture Reading

- What elements in this passage indicate that it is written as historical narrative?

  This passage can be immediately identified as historical narrative because it begins by presenting a temporal setting that can be determined by the existence of historical figures. Caesar Augustus was a historical person who ruled over a real Roman Empire, just as Quirinius was a historical person who oversaw Syria. Furthermore, the mention of other geographic locations and historical figures such as David shows how Luke is presenting the historical facts of the birth of Jesus Christ.

During the Video

Personification

- What is personification?

  Personification is defined as "the use of personal forms of description for impersonal objects, attributing human characteristics to inanimate things. An example of this can be found in Proverbs 1:20: "Wisdom cries aloud in the street, in the markets she raises her voice."

- What are two passages in which the line seems blurred between historical narrative and the personification that is commonly found in poetry?

  In Numbers 22, Balaam's donkey speaks after seeing the angel of the Lord, turning off the road, and being beaten. In Genesis 3, the serpent talks in the garden in order to tempt Eve. Both these accounts could be seen as examples of personification. Yet they take place in historical-narrative settings, and it is clear that Scripture's intention is to communicate supernatural occurrences.

- What crisis is related to questions about the presence of personification in historical narratives?

  The crisis related to these questions is over whether the Bible can be trusted in its presentation of historical facts. The resurrection of Jesus Christ is itself a historical fact. It has taken place in space and time. If certain parts of the Bible cannot be trusted, then this calls into question its claims that have eternal significance.

Historical Narrative

- What are some of the normal features of historical narrative?

  Some of the normal features of historical narrative are the presence of temporal settings, geographic locations, historical figures, prose style, genealogies, and the absence of a plainly stated moral lesson.

- Who bears the burden of proof when different literary forms are present in historical narrative and a passage's historicity is questioned?

  Sometimes different literary forms occur in historical narratives, such as the parables found in the Gospels. When many literary features are present in a historical narrative, the burden of proof falls on the one who challenges the historicity of the passage as a whole to differentiate these features and how they are being used.

After the Video

- What natural conclusion follows from rejection of a talking serpent in Genesis 3 as historically unbelievable?

  The account of the serpent's speaking in the garden has caused some to assert that such an account proves the very beginning of the Bible to be unhistorical and mythical in nature. This then naturally extends to questioning the reality of the fall and even the existence of a historical Adam and Eve.

- What might be the problem of the person who is skeptical that the account of the fall is historical? How would you try to convince the person otherwise?

  The idea of the serpent's speaking causes some to question the theological foundations of the entire Bible. The problem in this case may be one of unbelief. Its root cause may be in the rejection of a supernatural Creator who has the capacity to also bring about the supernatural.

- Why is it critical that we defend the historicity of the Bible?

  We must defend the Bible's historicity because the historical dimension of Christianity is the center of any controversy with the faith. The Christian faith is intimately tied to history because it narrates the history of our redemption through events. For this reason, the historical claims of Christianity are nonnegotiable, and as real, historical people, we need the real, historical redemption found only in Jesus Christ.

REVIEW QUIZ

Lesson 6

1. **A.**
Though personification can be present in historical narrative, it most often occurs in Hebrew poetry. Other biblical genres such as wisdom and apocalyptic literature also feature personification because of their poetic elements.

2. **C.**
Some label the account of Balaam's donkey as a fable, a literary genre that uses animals to teach moral lessons. The talking donkey would then be understood as an example of personification, even though the scene is narrated in prose and contains other historical elements.

3. **C.**
Barth replied, "What did the snake say?" when he was asked, "Did the snake speak?" This was a way of deflecting the question and shifting focus to the theological content of the snake's speech. But a straightforward answer to this question is vitally important to address people's need to know whether the Bible can be trusted.

4. **C.**
Historical narrative does not contain explicit moral lessons, though there may be lessons to derive from the text and moral lessons can appear embedded in historical narratives. Jesus' parables in the Gospels are a prime example of the latter.

5. **A.**
While elements in the early chapters of Genesis confront antisupernatural biases, clear historical features also appear. The early chapters of Genesis contain genealogy, geographical features, and prose. Furthermore, other biblical writers corroborate these chapters of Genesis as history.

6. **C.**
The Christian faith is tied to history and rests on such historical claims as the resurrection of Christ. This is why historical narrative in particular is center stage for conflict surrounding the faith and why we must defend the historical accuracy of the Bible.

7

Reading the Bible Existentially

INTRODUCTION

Many people read Scripture as though it were a collection of rules to be obeyed or facts to be memorized, but the Bible isn't a lifeless book. We must come to it as impassioned people because when we read the Bible, we can expect it to speak to us. In this lesson, Dr. Sproul opens up a way of reading the Bible that connects with the real-life humanity of its people and brings its drama to life.

LEARNING GOALS

When you have finished this lesson, you should be able to:

- Explain what it means to read the Bible existentially and how it opens us up to deeper involvement with the lives of God's people
- Approach the Bible with a desire to engage with it personally
- Better understand the nature of biblical narrative

KEY IDEAS

- We ought to be a people who are personally and passionately involved in our act of reading Scripture.
- We become personally engaged with the Bible by reading it existentially, bridging the gap between ourselves and the culture to which it was written.
- Reading existentially involves reading between the lines of biblical narrative to look for the drama already in the Bible.

REFLECTION & DISCUSSION QUESTIONS

Before the Video

What Do You Think?

Take a moment to answer the following questions. They will prepare you for the lecture.

- When you hear the word *existential*, what first comes to mind?

- What is a biblical narrative that has particularly come alive for you?

Scripture Reading

When they came to the place of which God had told him, Abraham built the altar there and laid the wood in order and bound Isaac his son and laid him on the altar, on top of the wood. Then Abraham reached out his hand and took the knife to slaughter his son. But the angel of the LORD called to him from heaven and said, "Abraham, Abraham!" And he said, "Here I am." He said, "Do not lay your hand on the boy or do anything to him, for now I know that you fear God, seeing you have not withheld your son, your only son, from me."

—Genesis 22:9–12

- What elements of this biblical narrative should pull you into its drama?

During the Video

Answer the following questions while you watch the video. They will guide you through the lecture.

Reading between the Lines *0:00–12:21*

- What does it mean to read the Bible "existentially"?

- What is an inappropriate way to approach the Bible?

- Where did Søren Kierkegaard read between the lines to find the drama in Abraham's call to sacrifice his son Isaac?

Finding the Drama *12:21–27:45*

- What is surprisingly not mentioned in the account of Nadab and Abihu in Leviticus 10?

- What does looking for the drama in a biblical narrative prevent?

After the Video

Answer the following questions after you have finished the lecture. They will help you identify and summarize the major points.

- What is a way to become more involved in biblical narrative? In what sense must we be cautious when employing this method?

  If you are in a group, have the members bring to mind and share biblical narratives that have been particularly impactful. Invite them to respond to the following question: What was it about the story or your experience that made it resonate with you?

- How does reading the Bible existentially differ from the existential methods of interpretation discussed in the third lesson?

  If you are in a group, have the members discuss why it is important that, regardless of our emotional state or intentions when we read the Bible, it is understood to be the Word of God. Ask the group how such a mentality might make us open to encouragement or correction.

- How would you respond to someone who said that he or she was bored by the Bible? How would you try to convince the person otherwise?

  If you are in a group, have the members read Daniel 2. Have them take turns reading aloud, encouraging them to bring out the drama in the text by how they read it.

PRAYER

Commit what you have learned from God's Word in this lesson to prayer.

- Praise God for His work in the lives of His people narrated for us in the Bible.
- Confess any times you've approached the Bible as though it were only a book of facts.

- Thank God for what He has done in your life through His Word, showing you how the Bible is a life-giving book.
- Ask God to continue to conform you to the image of Christ through the power of the Holy Spirit in your continued study of Scripture.

REVIEW QUIZ

Use these multiple-choice questions to measure what you learned from this lesson.

1. What philosopher said that there are three stages along life's way?
   a. Albert Camus
   b. Jean-Paul Sartre
   c. Søren Kierkegaard
   d. Friedrich Nietzsche
2. What is a purpose of reading the Bible existentially?
   a. To be personally affected by it
   b. To acquire objective facts about God
   c. To apply philosophical categories to it
   d. To analyze and dissect the Bible as literature
3. Reading the Bible existentially means employing the existential method of interpretation.
   a. True
   b. False
4. What biblical account is the focus of Søren Kierkegaard's *Fear and Trembling*?
   a. The death of Nadab and Abihu
   b. The garden of Gethsemane
   c. The sacrifice of Isaac
   d. The laws for cleansing lepers
5. It is important to distance ourselves from the Bible's stories so that we can objectively interpret them.
   a. True
   b. False
6. What does reading the Bible existentially *not* entail?
   a. Reading between the lines of a narrative
   b. Applying the Bible to real-life circumstances
   c. Interpreting the Bible in a purely subjective manner
   d. Identifying with the humanity of the people of the Bible

Answer Key—Reading the Bible Existentially

REFLECTION & DISCUSSION QUESTIONS

Before the Video

What Do You Think?

These are personal questions. The answers should be based on your own knowledge and experience.

Scripture Reading

- What elements of this biblical narrative should pull you into its drama?

  God tested Abraham by calling him to sacrifice his only son, Isaac. In this narrow section of that story, Abraham reaches the place that God had told him of and where he must build an altar, knowing that it is the one on which he would offer up his son. He binds his son, and just as he is raising his knife, at the greatest point of tension, the angel of the Lord speaks. The relationship of Abraham and Isaac, Abraham's faith in God, and all the actions that live out that faith build up the drama in such a way that it is one of the Bible's most tense and climactic moments.

During the Video

Reading between the Lines

- What does it mean to read the Bible "existentially"?

  Reading the Bible existentially is not inherently connected to the philosophy of existentialism, though it does bring us into direct, personal, and intimate engagement with the biblical text, such that we can apply it to our lives. In this sense, our reading of the Bible becomes existential because it becomes immediately applicable to our lives.

- What is an inappropriate way to approach the Bible?

  Dr. Sproul emphasized that one inappropriate way to approach the Bible is with the intention of remaining aloof from its message. We are not to reduce the Bible to an objective source of facts merely to be dissected, categorized, or even committed to memory. The Bible is a book filled with life, and it should affect our lives.

- Where did Søren Kierkegaard read between the lines to find the drama in Abraham's call to sacrifice his son Isaac?

  Genesis 22 narrates the account of Abraham's faithfulness in bringing Isaac before God as a sacrifice. Kierkegaard made this passage the focus of his philosophical work Fear and Trembling. *In order to process what Abraham was experiencing,*

Kierkegaard focused on the seemingly mundane line "Abraham rose early in the morning" (v. 3). He believed that perhaps Abraham's faith coupled with his profound anguish prompted his early rising.

Finding the Drama

- What is surprisingly not mentioned in the account of Nadab and Abihu in Leviticus 10?

  Leviticus 10 narrates the death of Nadab and Abihu for bringing an unauthorized offering before God. Surprisingly, the narrative does not mention anything about Aaron's immediate reaction to the death of his sons. There is a gap in the narrative before Moses tells Aaron the word from the Lord. Only then do we find out that "Aaron held his peace" (v. 3).

- What does looking for the drama in a biblical narrative prevent?

  People often say that the Bible is boring. Nothing could be further from the truth. Looking for the drama in the Bible uncovers how it is the most dramatic book ever written, filled with the stories of real people experiencing the full range of human emotions. For this reason, looking for the drama already in the Bible prevents it from ever becoming boring.

After the Video

- What is a way to become more involved in biblical narrative? In what sense must we be cautious when employing this method?

  Dr. Sproul commended a process of reading between the lines of a biblical narrative, which is usually sparse on details. Reading between the lines is a way of finding the drama in the story and identifying with the humanity of its characters. One precaution must be taken, however. We must not take too much license with the biblical text and fall victim to subjective interpretation. We can simply acknowledge the humanity of the people in the Bible in order to imagine how they felt.

- How does reading the Bible existentially differ from the existential methods of interpretation discussed in the third lesson?

  No matter how you approach the Bible, it is the objective and true Word of God. Reading the Bible existentially can bring you into the story so that its history comes alive for you in a meaningful way. On the other hand, the existential method of interpretation denies the objectivity of God's Word and its historical nature, allowing for the Bible to become the Word of God only when it meets us in our existential experience.

- How would you respond to someone who said that he or she was bored by the Bible? How would you try to convince the person otherwise?

  Although the answer to this question is subjective, this lesson has been, in a sense, an exercise to show how truly alive the Bible is. Many of the techniques Dr. Sproul used to dramatize the text could be employed, as well as a straightforward summary of the real-world stories in the Bible that span the full range of human emotion and cover such weighty themes as sin and redemption.

REVIEW QUIZ

Lesson 7

1. **C.**
   Nietzsche and Kierkegaard heavily influenced the existentialist movement of the twentieth century, as exemplified by such philosophers as Camus and Sartre. It was Kierkegaard who theorized that there are three stages in a person's life.

2. **A.**
   Although reading the Bible existentially involves a careful reading of literary features in the Bible, we do not come to the Bible merely to analyze or dissect it, or even to acquire facts about God. The Bible is not a textbook in this sense. We come to it to be changed by it.

3. **B.**
   The existential method of interpretation denies the objectivity of the Bible, allowing it to become the Word of God only when it speaks directly in one's existential experience. Reading the Bible existentially, however, is merely an approach to reading the Bible in an intimate and personal way.

4. **C.**
   Kierkegaard used the account of Abraham's would-be sacrifice of Isaac as a starting place for his work Fear and Trembling. *Dr. Sproul used Kierkegaard only as an example of someone who read the Bible existentially with an eye for the drama already in the text.*

5. **B.**
   While objectivity is heralded as an admirable quality, the idea of coming to the Bible as a purely disinterested observer disregards the Bible as the living and active Word of God. Whenever we read the Bible, we should remember that we are studying the very Word of God.

6. **C.**
   One of Dr. Sproul's warnings was that reading the Bible existentially is not license to read meaning into the text that isn't there. It is not a warrant for subjective interpretation. Reading the Bible existentially seeks to understand God's Word in an objective sense through a personal and intimate reading of the text.

8

The Historical Narrative

INTRODUCTION

Scripture provides us with all we need for faith and practice and is full of examples of godly men and women who lived lives of faith and integrity. What can be learned from their lives to benefit ours? In this lesson, Dr. Sproul demonstrates how to interpret historical narrative responsibly and shows how invalid conclusions about morality are often reached using the Bible's history.

LEARNING GOALS

When you have finished this lesson, you should be able to:

- Interpret the historical narrative of the Bible responsibly, allowing Scripture to interpret Scripture
- Provide negative examples for the importance of interpreting historical narrative by the didactic portions of Scripture

KEY IDEAS

- Historical narrative must be interpreted by the didactic.
- The Bible's historical narratives record events, whereas its didactic literature records the meaning of events.
- Scripture must interpret Scripture. We ought not draw conclusions from historical narratives that are counter to Scripture's explicit didactic teachings.

REFLECTION & DISCUSSION QUESTIONS

Before the Video

What Do You Think?

Take a moment to answer the following questions. They will prepare you for the lecture.

- What are some events in the Bible that could lead us to false conclusions about what is pleasing to God?

- Are historical events morally neutral? How can we evaluate them?

Scripture Reading

For to this you have been called, because Christ also suffered for you, leaving you an example, so that you might follow in his steps. He committed no sin, neither was deceit found in his mouth. When he was reviled, he did not revile in return; when he suffered, he did not threaten, but continued entrusting himself to him who judges justly. He himself bore our sins in his body on the tree, that we might die to sin and live to righteousness. By his wounds you have been healed.

—1 Peter 2:21–24

- What historical events does Peter mention? How does he interpret their meaning?

During the Video

Answer the following questions while you watch the video. They will guide you through the lecture.

Interpreting the Historical by the Didactic — *0:00–8:45*

- What does the word *didactic* mean?

- What is a general way to delineate the difference between a gospel and an epistle?

- What danger is avoided by interpreting the historical by the didactic?

Dangerous Conclusions — *8:45–27:08*

- What is a dangerous conclusion to draw from Abraham's near-sacrifice of Isaac?

- What is a dangerous conclusion to make about God's creating man in His own image?

- What is a dangerous conclusion to make related to Jesus' acts during His earthly ministry?

- What is a dangerous conclusion to draw about the example of the early church?

After the Video

Answer the following questions after you have finished the lecture. They will help you identify and summarize the major points.

- Why is the cross of Jesus Christ a perfect example of the need to interpret the historical by the didactic?

  If you are in a group, have the members read Mark 14:53–65. Invite them to respond to the following questions: How many different viewpoints are there about the identity of Jesus and His earthly ministry? Where does didactic teaching appear in this gospel passage?

- What are some interpretive principles that can be drawn from the examples in this lesson?

  If you are in a group, have the members discuss the importance of using Scripture to interpret Scripture. Ask them what the tendency to position different authors of Scripture against one another misses about the nature of Scripture.

- Which of the dangerous conclusions outlined in this lesson have you fallen into in the past or do you notice how easy it would be to fall into? Why is it so dangerous?

  If you are in a group, have the members read Acts 1:8; 8:14–17; 10:44. Then have them discuss how Acts 1:8 helps explain the significance of the unity of the church that Dr. Sproul emphasized in relation to the Holy Spirit in Acts.

PRAYER

Commit what you have learned from God's Word in this lesson to prayer.

- Praise God for providing in His Word both history and its interpretation.
- Confess any tendency you have to study God's Word in a shallow manner.
- Thank God for His Holy Spirit, who helps us interpret Scripture.
- Ask God to protect you from drawing erroneous conclusions about His Word.

REVIEW QUIZ

Use these multiple-choice questions to measure what you learned from this lesson.

1. What must we use to interpret historical narrative?
   a. The didactic
   b. The exegetical
   c. The prophetic
   d. The mysterious

2. The primary purpose of historical narrative is to tell the story.
   a. True
   b. False

3. What's an example of something that we are *not* to imitate from Christ's life?
   a. His love for God
   b. His love for neighbor
   c. His faithfulness in prayer
   d. His circumcision according to the law

4. What is a good way of evaluating the acceptability of a biblical character's actions?
   a. Looking at the outcome of his actions
   b. Judging his actions based on our moral decisions
   c. Considering the cultural influences of his actions
   d. Finding out whether his actions are commended by God

5. It is wise to adhere to all the practices of the New Testament because it was uniquely inspired by the Holy Spirit.
   a. True
   b. False

6. What is *not* a valid principle deduced from this lesson?
   a. Scripture must be used to interpret Scripture.
   b. The didactic takes priority over the historical in matters of doctrine.
   c. A person's statement in a historical narrative determines meaning.
   d. Not every action performed by Christ is necessarily to be imitated.

Answer Key—The Historical Narrative

REFLECTION & DISCUSSION QUESTIONS

Before the Video

What Do You Think?

These are personal questions. The answers should be based on your own knowledge and experience.

Scripture Reading

- What historical events does Peter mention? How does he interpret their meaning?

  Peter names a number of events centered on Jesus Christ: His sinless life, the manner in which He suffered, and His death on the cross. Peter gives a plain interpretation of the significance of Jesus' death, in particular, when he highlights that through His death He bore our sins, resulting in our dying to sin and our living to righteousness.

During the Video

Interpreting the Historical by the Didactic

- What does the word *didactic* mean?

  The word didactic *comes from the Greek verb* didaskō, *which means "to teach." In Greek, a* didaskalos *is thus a "teacher." So didactic literature is the genre of literature with the primary purpose of teaching.*

- What is a general way to delineate the difference between a gospel and an epistle?

  The Gospels do contain teaching and Jesus' clear statements about the significance of His life and death, but a general way of thinking about the Gospels is that they present historical events. The Epistles, on the other hand, provide the inspired interpretation of those events.

- What danger is avoided by interpreting the historical by the didactic?

  When we interpret the historical narrative of the Bible with the didactic literature of the Bible, we free ourselves from drawing false inferences from raw facts. We need not only the historical facts but also their divine interpretation, lest we pit the Bible's narrative against its teaching.

Dangerous Conclusions

- What is a dangerous conclusion to draw from Abraham's near-sacrifice of Isaac?

  In Genesis 22:12, the angel of the Lord stops Abraham from sacrificing Isaac, saying, "Do not lay your hand on the boy or do anything to him, for now I know that you fear God, seeing you have not withheld your son, your only son, from me." It is dangerous to conclude from this passage that God did not know what Abraham was going to do. Didactic portions of Scripture clearly teach that God knows all things.

- What is a dangerous conclusion to make about God's creating man in His own image?

  Genesis 1:27 tells us, "God created man in his own image." Mormons falsely conclude that this means God must have a body because people are embodied. Didactic portions of Scripture clearly teach that God is a spirit (John 4:24).

- What is a dangerous conclusion to make related to Jesus' acts during His earthly ministry?

  A dangerous conclusion is looking at the earthly ministry of Christ in too rigid a manner, assuming that Christians must do exactly the same things He did. While it is true that we are elsewhere called to imitate Him, a distinction should be made between Jesus as Messiah and Lord of the church and ourselves.

- What is a dangerous conclusion to draw about the example of the early church?

  In Acts 4, we learn that the early church "had everything in common" (v. 32), which could lead some to conclude that having communal possessions is a perpetual command for the church. False inferences may also be drawn from the book of Acts related to the Holy Spirit and spiritual gifts.

After the Video

- Why is the cross of Jesus Christ a perfect example of the need to interpret the historical by the didactic?

  On the surface, the crucifixion of Jesus Christ may look only like the death of a man who was convicted as a criminal by the Roman government and who committed blasphemy and suffered a cursed death, according to the Jewish authorities. The Gospels report that many interpreted His death along these exact lines. In the New Testament, not only do we have the record of these historic events, but we also have the inspired interpretation of these events, which we find most explicitly in the Epistles.

- What are some interpretive principles that can be drawn from the examples in this lesson?

  The number one principle from this lesson is that the historical must be interpreted by the didactic. Subsumed under this principle, specific principles could be noted: We must not set one portion of Scripture against another. We must understand the relationship of the Gospels and the Epistles. We must not draw conclusions from narratives only. We must not be compelled to model our behavior after Christ's in an exact, legalistic way. We must not imitate biblical figures without considering God's perspective, imitating what He praises and avoiding what He condemns. We must be careful about the conclusions we draw about the early church.

- Which of the dangerous conclusions outlined in this lesson have you fallen into in the past or do you notice would be easy to fall into? Why is it so dangerous?

  The answer to this question takes into consideration the multiple examples of ways that false conclusions can be drawn from not interpreting the historical by the didactic. An example is the temptation to determine one's theology of regeneration based on the activity of the Holy Spirit with the Samaritans in Acts 8 alone.

REVIEW QUIZ

Lesson 8

1. **A.**
   The didactic portions of Scripture reveal its explicit teachings. Instead of allowing historical facts to determine our ethics or doctrine, we need to look to Scripture's most explicit teachings as divine interpretation of biblical events.

2. **A.**
   Historical narrative is designed to communicate facts. Sometimes historical narrative is accompanied by divine interpretation of events, but historical narrative's primary purpose is to tell us what happened.

3. **D.**
   While Jesus Christ is our perfect example, there are many dimensions of His life that we are neither able nor called to imitate. One example is His circumcision according to the law. If we rigidly applied the principle that we ought to imitate Christ in all things, we would submit ourselves to a mode of legalism that He has freed us from.

4. **D.**
   There are many ways to evaluate someone's actions in the Bible, but only one of these is a reliable way to determine whether they are worthy of imitation: Did God praise the person's actions? Or did God condemn them? If Scripture is not explicit in stating this, God's judgment is still the standard, for we have His standard of judgment in His law.

5. **B.**
   The Holy Spirit is always at work in Christ's church, and one could certainly point to instances in the Epistles of the New Testament that plainly condemn sin in the early church, just as sin in the church should be condemned today.

6. **C.**
   This lesson has worked through the implications of the principle that historical narrative must be interpreted by the didactic. It warned of the danger of drawing conclusions from narrative alone, even when it comes to following Christ's example. A person's speech in a narrative is still part of a narrative, and we have to determine who is speaking and, through the didactic portions of Scripture, determine whether that person's evaluation of a situation is correct.

9

The Explicit & the Implicit

INTRODUCTION

Throughout church history, many Scripture passages have attracted a variety of strange—and wrong—interpretations. How do we avoid the error of drawing something from Scripture that is simply not there? What principle do we call on to guide us in our efforts to understand God's Word? In this lesson, Dr. Sproul explains the importance of drawing our doctrine from the explicit statements of Scripture.

LEARNING GOALS

When you have finished this lesson, you should be able to:

- Understand the importance and necessity of drawing inferences from Scripture
- Recognize how easy it is to draw false inferences in Scripture
- Provide examples of why we must study words in context

KEY IDEAS

- The implicit is to be interpreted by the explicit. The obscure or the difficult is to be interpreted in light of that which is plain and clear.
- It is important for us to draw reasonable inferences from Scripture that follow from necessary consequence.
- Context must be used to determine the meaning of words, lest we import meaning into a passage of Scripture that is not there.

REFLECTION & DISCUSSION QUESTIONS

Before the Video

What Do You Think?

Take a moment to answer the following questions. They will prepare you for the lecture.

- Using Scripture to interpret Scripture is vital. What are ways that we may misuse even this principle?

- What helpful resources do you turn to when studying the Bible?

Scripture Reading

"Hear, O Israel: The LORD our God, the LORD is one."

—Deuteronomy 6:4

In the beginning was the Word, and the Word was with God, and the Word was God.

—John 1:1

- What is explicitly taught in these verses?

During the Video

Answer the following questions while you watch the video. They will guide you through the lecture.

The Principle *0:00–3:55*

- What is another way of stating the principle that the implicit must be interpreted in light of the explicit?

- What is an example of the necessity of inferences? When do inferences become a problem?

Case Studies *3:55–20:44*

- What unnecessary inference do people make about the disciples' encounter with the resurrected Christ in the book of John?

- What unnecessary inference do people make from Paul's teaching about head coverings in 1 Corinthians 11? How do people support this interpretation?

- What inference do people attempt to make from John 3:16? How is this resolved by John 6:44?

The Meaning of Words *20:44–26:45*

- Why are the verb *to save* and the word *salvation* examples of why we must be careful about how we handle words in the Bible?

- What must be used to determine the meaning of a word in the Bible?

After the Video

Answer the following questions after you have finished the lecture. They will help you identify and summarize the major points.

- We must be cautious when we draw inferences from Scripture. Why is it necessary, though, to draw inferences? How does this necessity extend to applying Scripture?

  If you are in a group, have the members discuss their goals when they sit down to study the Bible. Ask them: What are they hoping God will do? How do they seek to apply Scripture to their lives?

- The doctrine of the Trinity is taught implicitly in Scripture. Since the implicit is to be interpreted by the explicit, should we question the doctrine of the Trinity? If not, why not?

  If you are in a group, have the members read Genesis 1:1, Job 33:4, and Colossians 1:15–19. How do these verses work with Deuteronomy 6:4 in affirming the doctrine of the Trinity as a valid inference from Scripture?

- Earlier in this teaching series, it was argued that any given biblical text can have only one intended meaning. In this lesson, we learned that words can have multiple meanings. How, then, can it be argued that a specific biblical text has only one meaning?

  If you are in a group, have the members discuss what they consider to be the most important issues raised in this lesson.

PRAYER

Commit what you have learned from God's Word in this lesson to prayer.

- Praise God for revealing who He is as Father, Son, and Spirit.
- Confess areas of your life where you are neglecting a clear teaching of Scripture.
- Thank God for His gifting the church with His Spirit to interpret Scripture.
- Ask God to give you wisdom when you make inferences from Scripture.

REVIEW QUIZ

Use these multiple-choice questions to measure what you learned from this lesson.

1. What doctrine is an example of the importance of making inferences from Scripture?
   a. Sin
   b. Creation
   c. Justification
   d. The Trinity
2. In careful exegesis, inferences drawn from the implicit in a text should be used to challenge the explicit meaning of a text elsewhere.
   a. True
   b. False
3. What theologically loaded word is an example of why we must be careful with biblical words?
   a. Lord
   b. Prayer
   c. Resurrection
   d. Forgiveness
4. What phrase refers to the descendants of Seth?
   a. Sons of God
   b. Sons of Abraham
   c. Sons of Adam
   d. Sons of man
5. In Greek and in Hebrew, just as in English, words can often have more than one meaning.
   a. True
   b. False
6. What should we first look at in interpreting a word's meaning in Scripture?
   a. Concordance
   b. Dictionary
   c. Commentary
   d. Context

Answer Key—The Explicit & the Implicit

REFLECTION & DISCUSSION QUESTIONS

Before the Video

What Do You Think?

These are personal questions. The answers should be based on your own knowledge and experience.

Scripture Reading

- What is explicitly taught in these verses?

  The verse from Deuteronomy explicitly teaches that the Lord is one in essence and that He is God alone. The verse from John explicitly teaches that the Word also is God. From these two passages, a necessary inference must be made, one that will be further discussed in this lesson.

During the Video

The Principle

- What is another way of stating the principle that the implicit must be interpreted in light of the explicit?

  Another way of stating the principle is that the obscure or difficult is to be interpreted in light of that which is plain or clear. That is the essential difference between what is explicitly stated and what is only implicitly stated. The explicit is what Scripture directly states, whereas the implicit is not stated directly.

- What is an example of the necessity of inferences? When do inferences become a problem?

  The doctrine of the Trinity is an example of why inferences must be made from Scripture. The Bible explicitly teaches that there is one God, but the Father, Son, and Holy Spirit are all attributed with divinity. Therefore, an inference is made about the Trinity. This inference has a necessary conclusion. Inferences are problematic, however, when they conflict with what Scripture explicitly teaches elsewhere.

Case Studies

- What unnecessary inference do people make about the disciples' encounter with the resurrected Christ in the book of John?

  John 20:26 says, "Although the doors were locked, Jesus came and stood among them and said, 'Peace be with you.'" An unnecessary inference from this passage is that Jesus is able to pass through walls in His resurrected body. This is a possible inference, but it is not a necessary conclusion because there may be other explanations for John's detail about the locked door.

- What unnecessary inference do people make from Paul's teaching about head coverings in 1 Corinthians 11? How do people support this interpretation?

  First Corinthians 11 contains an obscure phrase: "because of the angels" (v. 10). The meaning of this phrase is notoriously unclear. Some have taken it to refer to an angel's attraction to women. To reach this conclusion, some appeal to Genesis 6, interpreting this passage as describing angelic and human sexual relations, which is not a necessary inference from the text.

- What inference do people attempt to make from John 3:16? How is this resolved by John 6:44?

  John 3:16 tells us that "whoever believes" in the Son will have eternal life. The language of this passage provides a possible inference that anyone has the moral ability to believe in Jesus Christ, but this is not a necessary inference from the text. It is not something the words demand we infer. It does, however, teach explicitly that whoever believes can be certain of everlasting life. In John 6:44, Jesus says, "No one can come to me unless the Father who sent me draws him." Here, Jesus clearly addresses the question of man's moral ability to come to Him. By allowing Scripture to interpret Scripture, we see that John 3:16 does not teach that anyone has the ability in himself to trust in Christ.

The Meaning of Words

- Why are the verb *to save* and the word *salvation* examples of why we must be careful about how we handle words in the Bible?

  The verb to save *occurs in multiple tenses throughout the Bible to teach us the past, present, future, and ongoing implications of our salvation. If we were to isolate an instance where the Bible refers to our future salvation, for instance, we might wrongly conclude something about our salvation now. The word* salvation *itself is also used to denote different sorts of salvation, such as being healed from disease, and does not always relate to the salvation that comes from faith in Jesus Christ.*

- What must be used to determine the meaning of a word in the Bible?

  In order for us not to transfer the meaning of a word in one passage of Scripture to another, though the same word is used, we must heed each passage's context.

After the Video

- We must be cautious when we draw inferences from Scripture. Why is it necessary, though, to draw inferences? How does this necessity extend to applying Scripture?

It is important for us to draw inferences from Scripture. It's a necessary practice, but we must be sure that our inferences are valid. Dr. Sproul used the doctrine of the Trinity as an example of why we must make inferences from Scripture. The Trinity is a valid inference from the implicit teaching of Scripture. When it comes to applying Scripture to our lives, it doesn't speak directly about our circumstances, so we must also make inferences to put its principles to action.

- The doctrine of the Trinity is taught implicitly in Scripture. Since the implicit is to be interpreted by the explicit, should we question the doctrine of the Trinity? If not, why not?

  Though there is not one verse that proves the doctrine of the Trinity in Scripture, the doctrine is a valid inference from Scripture. In the case of the doctrine of the Trinity, multiple places in Scripture that explicitly affirm the divinity of the Father, Son, and Holy Spirit work together with passages that explicitly teach that there is only one God. Thus, the doctrine of the Trinity is deduced from Scripture's explicit teaching.

- Earlier in this teaching series, it was argued that any given biblical text can have only one intended meaning. In this lesson, we learned that words can have multiple meanings. How, then, can it be argued that a specific biblical text has only one meaning?

  This can be argued because we must use the context of any given biblical text to determine the meaning of its words. Rather than denying the truth that a passage of Scripture has one intended meaning, paying attention to a passage's context to discern the meaning of a word affirms it. While a word can have a range of meanings, it has only one intended meaning when an author uses it in a particular context.

REVIEW QUIZ

Lesson 9

1. **D.**
   Scripture explicitly affirms that there is only one God, yet it also ascribes divine titles and attributes to the Father, Son, and Holy Spirit. Therefore, an inference must be made. Though never stated explicitly in Scripture, the doctrine of the Trinity is a necessary conclusion from Scripture.

2. **B.**
   It must be remembered that the opposite is true because the explicit is what is plain or directly stated, whereas the implicit is not directly stated. Sometimes our inference may be a possible conclusion from a text but not a necessary conclusion.

3. **A.**
   Dr. Sproul used such theological words as salvation, sanctification, *and* Lord *as*

examples of why we must be careful when interpreting the meaning of words in Scripture. Lord *is used throughout the New Testament of Jesus, yet it does not mean that everyone who approached Him using this title understood who He truly was.* Lord *was an honorific title in that day. Elsewhere in the New Testament, however, the full theological import of this title as applied to Jesus is clear.*

4. **A.**
   Genesis 6 describes how "the sons of God saw that the daughters of man were attractive" (v. 2). Some have interpreted "sons of God" to refer to angelic beings. But "sons of God," as many commentators suggest, designates the godly line of Seth and "daughters of man" the ungodly line of Cain.

5. **A.**
   Words can have a range of meanings. This can be seen by studying the use of the word "salvation" in various places in Scripture. It does not always denote the salvific reality that comes from faith in Jesus Christ.

6. **D.**
   Even though the same word may be used in multiple places in Scripture, it does not necessarily mean the same thing in every place. In order to do justice to the meaning of a word, we must interpret it in the context in which it occurs. This is the first thing we should examine, and next we may look to different resources to help us in our studies.

10

Parallelisms

INTRODUCTION

We know that the Bible is the Word of God and, as such, does not contain contradictions, but what do we do with passages and statements that seem contradictory or impossible to explain? When we are confronted by these passages, we need to consider our methods of interpretation to be sure that we are approaching the Bible on its own terms. In this lesson, Dr. Sproul explains and teaches us to recognize the Hebrew poetic device of parallelism to help us in this task.

LEARNING GOALS

When you have finished this lesson, you should be able to:

- Understand basic literary features of Wisdom Literature and Hebrew poetry
- Recognize three different forms of parallelism that are found in the Bible
- Explain the types of law used in the Bible to help interpret proverbs

KEY IDEAS

- The three main forms of parallelism in the Bible are synonymous, antithetical, and synthetic parallelism.
- Parallelism is a feature of Hebrew poetry that, when recognized, can help us clarify a passage's meaning by allowing the plain to interpret the obscure.
- We must not confuse proverbial wisdom with moral absolutes.

REFLECTION & DISCUSSION QUESTIONS

Before the Video

What Do You Think?

Take a moment to answer the following questions. They will prepare you for the lecture.

- Do you find the poetic elements of Scripture inspiring or difficult? Are you more inclined to turn to the poetry found in Wisdom Literature or in the prophetic writings?

- How do you apply the book of Proverbs to your life? Do individual proverbs always prove true in every situation?

Scripture Reading

I am the LORD, and there is none else, there is no God beside me: I girded thee, though thou hast not known me: That they may know from the rising of the sun, and from the west, that there is none beside me. I am the LORD, and there is none else. I form the light, and create darkness: I make peace, and create evil: I the LORD do all these things.

—Isaiah 45:5–7 (KJV)

- What theological problem is brought out in the phrase "I make peace, and create evil"? What is the main point of this passage?

During the Video

Answer the following questions while you watch the video. They will guide you through the lecture.

Types of Parallelism *0:00–14:35*

- What is synonymous parallelism?

- What is antithetical parallelism?

- What is synthetic parallelism?

Interpreting Proverbs *14:35–26:21*

- What must we be able to do before we can interpret a proverb?

- What is a casuistic law?

- What is an apodictic law?

After the Video

Answer the following questions after you have finished the lecture. They will help you identify and summarize the major points.

- How did Dr. Sproul resolve the theological problem that arises from the translation of Isaiah 45:7 in the King James Version?

  If you are in a group, have the members read Matthew 7:7–8; 7:17–18; 23:5–10; Mark 3:24–25; 8:35; Luke 6:27–28; 12:49–51; 16:10. Have them classify these different types of parallelism.

- Apodictic law is the foundation of casuistic law. Explain this statement.
  How does this principle help you understand how to apply the Bible to your circumstances?

  If you are in a group, have the members read the Ten Commandments in Exodus 20 and discuss how they are able to address and to be applied to every circumstance of our lives.

- Do Proverbs 26:4 and 26:5 contradict each other? Why or why not?

  If you are in a group, have the members read Proverbs 22:6. Invite them to respond to the following question: How can understanding the different types of precepts in the Bible help you comfort someone who is struggling with a situation that doesn't seem to be working out according to this proverb?

PRAYER

Commit what you have learned from God's Word in this lesson to prayer.

- Praise God for the manifold ways in which He has revealed Himself in Scripture.
- Confess any slothfulness in your devotions to God.
- Thank God for the self-clarifying nature of His Word.
- Ask God for wisdom to apply the wisdom of Proverbs to your life.

REVIEW QUIZ

Use these multiple-choice questions to measure what you learned from this lesson.

1. What statement summarizes what G.C. Berkouwer called the "biblical a priori"?
   a. We must never call God the author of sin.
   b. We must never deny the existence of God.
   c. We must never downplay the role of Christ.
   d. We must never underestimate the power of sin.

2. What type of parallelism is used in Isaiah 45:7?
   a. Synonymous
   b. Antithetical
   c. Synthetic
   d. All of the above

3. What type of parallelism builds to a crescendo?
   a. Synonymous
   b. Antithetical
   c. Synthetic
   d. None of the above

4. The Ten Commandments are what type of law?
   a. Casuistic
   b. Apodictic
   c. Proverbial
   d. All of the above

5. Proverbs are moral absolutes in poetic form.
   a. True
   b. False

6. In what two biblical genres will you most likely find parallelism?
   a. Wisdom Literature and prophetic writings
   b. Prophetic writings and historical narrative
   c. Historical narrative and poetry
   d. Poetry and epistle

Answer Key—Parallelisms

REFLECTION & DISCUSSION QUESTIONS

Before the Video

What Do You Think?

These are personal questions. The answers should be based on your own knowledge and experience.

Scripture Reading

- What theological problem is brought out in the phrase "I make peace, and create evil"? What is the main point of this passage?

  The King James Version of Isaiah 45:7 states that God creates evil—but God is good, and He is not the author of evil. Modern translations help bring out the parallelism of this verse, which will be discussed in this lesson. Apart from this interpretive difficulty, the main point of the passage is plain. God alone is sovereign, and there is no other God.

During the Video

Types of Parallelism

- What is synonymous parallelism?

  Parallelism is a poetic device that sets two elements of Scripture in close proximity. In synonymous parallelism, these two elements convey the same idea but in a slightly different way. An example of synonymous parallelism is Proverbs 19:5: "A false witness will not go unpunished, and he who breathes out lies will not escape."

- What is antithetical parallelism?

  In antithetical parallelism, two elements of a parallel structure do not convey the same idea. Rather, they contrast with each other. An example of antithetical parallelism is Proverbs 13:10: "By insolence comes nothing but strife, but with those who take advice is wisdom."

- What is synthetic parallelism?

  In synthetic parallelism, two or more elements in a parallel structure are set in such a way that they build on one another and rise in a crescendo to round out a concept. An example of synthetic parallelism is Matthew 7:7: "Ask, and it will be given to you; seek, and you will find; knock, and it will be opened to you."

Interpreting Proverbs

- What must we be able to do before we can interpret a proverb?

  To interpret a proverb correctly, we must first be able to distinguish between three types of laws or principles that are found in Scripture: casuistic, apodictic, and proverbial laws. Once we know the difference between these laws, we can rightly understand and apply the wisdom of the Proverbs.

- What is a casuistic law?

  Casuistic law *refers to the many case laws found in Scripture that give guidance in judicial matters. Casuistic laws are usually accompanied by an* if-then *formula, such that if X happens, then Y. Examples of casuistic laws can be found especially in the books of Exodus, Leviticus, and Deuteronomy.*

- What is an apodictic law?

  Apodictic law *refers to the moral absolutes of Scripture. The greatest example of a set of apodictic laws is the Ten Commandments. The Ten Commandments follow the customary formula for apodictic law of "thou shalt" and "thou shalt not." Apodictic laws are the foundational principles on which casuistic laws are established.*

After the Video

- How did Dr. Sproul resolve the theological problem that arises from the translation of Isaiah 45:7 in the King James Version?

  Isaiah 45:7 reads, "I form the light, and create darkness: I make peace, and create evil: I the LORD do all these things" (KJV). Dr. Sproul resolved this issue by first demonstrating that this verse uses antithetical parallelism. "Light" is contrasted with "darkness," but "evil" does not correspond to "peace." One would expect "war" or "calamity" to better contrast with "peace." This is why modern translations handle this verse differently and do justice to the range of nuances in the Hebrew word for "evil." By recognizing the use of parallelism, Dr. Sproul used the clearer half of the parallel structure to interpret the obscure half.

- Apodictic law is the foundation of casuistic law. Explain this statement. How does this principle help you to understand how to apply the Bible to your circumstances?

  Apodictic law is the foundation of casuistic law. The moral absolutes of Scripture serve as the basis for Scripture's various case laws. In effect, the case laws of Scripture are the application of Scripture's moral absolutes. There is a correspondence between how the moral law works out through case laws and how the moral law should work out in our lives. Though Scripture does not detail every aspect of our experience, in applying Scripture, we must look to God's perfect law and depend on Him for the wisdom to live according to it. We might even use the Epistles as examples of how that law was applied in light of the gospel in the early church.

- Do Proverbs 26:4 and 26:5 contradict each other? Why or why not?

  At first glance, "Answer not a fool according to his folly . . ." and "Answer a fool according to his folly . . ." appear to be contradictory. Yet we must understand the nature of proverbs as general principles. They are not moral absolutes, but they are wisdom from the mind of God. We must use wisdom in applying them to our unique situations.

REVIEW QUIZ

Lesson 10

1. **A.**
   Related to the theological issue raised by Isaiah 45:7, God must never be called the author of sin and evil. G.C. Berkouwer called this principle the "biblical a priori." It is basic to Scripture that God did not create evil in the ultimate sense.

2. **B.**
   Isaiah 45:7 uses antithetical parallelism. This is how we know that "peace" does not correspond to "evil." Rather, we clearly see "light" contrasted with "darkness," so "peace" better contrasts with "calamity," as found in some modern translations.

3. **C.**
   Synthetic parallelism uses two or more elements that build on one another and rise in a crescendo. The effect of this type of parallelism is a completed concept. An example of synthetic parallelism is Matthew 7:7: "Ask, and it will be given to you; seek, and you will find; knock, and it will be opened to you."

4. **B.**
   Apodictic laws are Scripture's moral absolutes. Casuistic laws are found in the case laws of Scripture, and these are the application of moral absolutes. The epitome of Scripture's moral absolutes is found in the Ten Commandments.

5. **B.**
   People run into problems with biblical proverbs if they are seen as moral absolutes. One place that could cause issues is Proverbs 26:4–5. If these verses were seen as moral absolutes, then they would seem to contradict each other. But if they are seen as principles to guide our decisions in wisdom, then we understand that there is a situation for each one.

6. **A.**
   The examples used in this lesson for the different types of parallelism were taken from the Proverbs, the Gospels, and the book of the prophet Isaiah. With the exception of the Gospels, it is clear that we should expect to encounter parallelism in the Wisdom Literature and prophetic writings of Scripture. Poetry is the literary style of Wisdom Literature.

11

Scripture & Culture

INTRODUCTION

Knowing Scripture provides you with the tools and principles to properly interpret God's Word and apply its truth to your life, but one of the most important and most difficult topics in biblical interpretation is the relationship between Scripture and culture. In this lesson, Dr. Sproul outlines the twofold problem we face when interpreting the Bible and introduces the differences between principles and customs.

LEARNING GOALS

When you have finished this lesson, you should be able to:

- State the twofold problem we have when interpreting Scripture
- Define and give examples of principles and customs in Scripture
- Explain how the question of Scripture's relationship with culture interacts with one's view of the Bible

KEY IDEAS

- We must both understand the original meaning of Scripture and know how to apply it.
- The reality of division in the church demonstrates the importance of thinking about the modern-day application of biblical principles.
- We must understand the difference between a principle and a custom in Scripture because dismissing a biblical principle as a mere custom would be a serious offense against God.

REFLECTION & DISCUSSION QUESTIONS

Before the Video

What Do You Think?

Take a moment to answer the following questions. They will prepare you for the lecture.

- What are some issues that divide the church today? How is a person's understanding of Scripture related to them?

- What are some principles in Scripture? What are some customs?

Scripture Reading

On the following day, when they came from Bethany, he was hungry. And seeing in the distance a fig tree in leaf, he went to see if he could find anything on it. When he came to it, he found nothing but leaves, for it was not the season for figs. And he said to it, "May no one ever eat fruit from you again." And his disciples heard it.

—Mark 11:12–14

- What details in this passage may give us a hint why Jesus cursed the fig tree? What detail makes this difficult to understand?

During the Video

Answer the following questions while you watch the video. They will guide you through the lecture.

A Twofold Problem — *0:00–9:56*

- What twofold problem do we face when studying Scripture?

- What concept is illustrated by the stories about the African missionary and the inner city?

Case Study: Women in the Church — *9:56–16:12*

- What interpretive question is at the center of the debate over the role of women in church leadership?

- Even when people acknowledge the Bible's teaching about the role of women in the church, how is its teaching then dismissed?

Principles and Customs *16:12–27:40*

- What is a principle? What is a custom?

- If the Bible contains both principles and customs, what question do we then face?

After the Video

Answer the following questions after you have finished the lecture. They will help you identify and summarize the major points.

- How do the biblical and geographical contexts of Jesus' cursing the fig tree help us interpret the meaning of His action?

  If you are in a group, have the members read Mark 11:12–25. Then ask them the following question: Considering Dr. Sproul's interpretation of the object lesson of the fig tree, what is the significance of the placement of Jesus' cleansing of the temple in Mark 11:15–19?

- Some consider the Apostle Paul's views about women chauvinistic. How do such accusations betray a greater dilemma over the nature and application of Scripture?

  If you are in a group, have the members read Ephesians 5:22–33. Ask them to identify what language in this passage suggests that Paul had a high view of women.

- What danger is involved when considering whether something in Scripture is a principle or a custom?

  If you are in a group, have the members skim 1 Corinthians 5–11. Invite them to respond to the following questions: What practices and exhortations are clearly enduring principles? What practices and exhortations might be customary?

PRAYER

Commit what you have learned from God's Word in this lesson to prayer.

- Praise God as the One who knows the beginning from the end.
- Confess any tendency to dismiss or put off scriptural principles.
- Thank God that Jesus Christ is the same yesterday, today, and forever.
- Ask God to help you to be not only a hearer but also a doer of His Word.

REVIEW QUIZ

Use these multiple-choice questions to measure what you learned from this lesson.

1. What term summarizes the second part of our twofold problem when studying the Bible?
   a. Exegesis
   b. Interpretation
   c. Historical analysis
   d. Application

2. What type of law from the previous lesson is by nature most like a principle and not customary or situational?
   a. Casuistic
   b. Apodictic
   c. Proverbial
   d. All of the above

3. We are faced with the responsibility to distinguish between principle and custom in Scripture.
   a. True
   b. False

4. What purpose did the topic of women in the church serve in this lesson?
   a. To expose liberal views of Scripture
   b. To show how culture can overrule Scripture
   c. To help us see the difficulties involved in applying the Bible
   d. To resolve the tensions caused by this divisive issue

5. It is dangerous both to dismiss a principle as a custom and to raise a custom to the level of a principle.
   a. True
   b. False

6. What was *not* a possible example of a customary practice mentioned by Dr. Sproul?
   a. Jesus' foot-washing in John 13
   b. Jesus' instruction to His missionary disciples in Luke 10
   c. Jesus' commands about the Lord's Supper in Luke 22
   d. None of the above

Answer Key—Scripture & Culture

REFLECTION & DISCUSSION QUESTIONS

Before the Video

What Do You Think?

These are personal questions. The answers should be based on your own knowledge and experience.

Scripture Reading

- What details in this passage may give us a hint why Jesus cursed the fig tree? What detail makes this difficult to understand?

  In this passage, we read that Jesus was hungry and that the fig tree was "in leaf," so the reason Jesus went to it was that He expected to find something to eat. These two details hint at why Jesus was inclined to curse the tree. The detail about its not being the "season for figs" makes His cursing of the tree difficult to understand. Mark 11:20–25 explicitly gives us the reason why it was cursed. Dr. Sproul will focus on this passage in more detail in this lesson.

During the Video

A Two-Fold Problem

- What twofold problem do we face when studying Scripture?

  The first problem we have when studying Scripture is the interpretation of its meaning in its historical context. The second problem is applying it to our lives. Both of these are considered problems because we must overcome the thousands of years that separate us from Scripture's original audience.

- What concept is illustrated by the stories about the African missionary and the inner city?

  In both these stories, one main point was stressed: we face the problem of transcultural communication when studying the Bible. These two modern-day examples of this problem drive home the difficulty we face of understanding another culture. Our everyday experience, to an extent, is different from the everyday experience of the people of the Bible.

Case Study: Women in the Church

- What interpretive question is at the center of the debate over the role of women in church leadership?

  When conservative and liberal Christians agree that the Bible plainly speaks about women's role in the leadership of the church, the question about interpreting its restrictions then becomes whether they apply to women today as they did in the first century.

- Even when people acknowledge the Bible's teaching about the role of women in the church, how is its teaching then dismissed?

  When the Bible's teaching about women's role in the church is acknowledged to be clear, people still dismiss its teaching by asserting that it does not apply beyond its cultural context or by asserting that its teaching reflects the chauvinistic prejudices of the Apostle Paul.

Principles and Customs

- What is a principle? What is a custom?

  A principle is a teaching, admonition, or precept that is transcultural, meaning that it applies to all people in all ages. A custom is a principle governing people at a particular time and in a particular locality.

- If the Bible contains both principles and customs, what question do we then face?

  If the Bible contains both principles and customs, then we face the question of determining between principle and custom. We have to determine what is normative for every Christian in every age and what was applicable to God's people at only a certain point in history.

After the Video

- How do the biblical and geographical contexts of Jesus' cursing the fig tree help us interpret the meaning of His action?

  Jesus' action of cursing the fig tree has been criticized by some as capricious because He cursed it for not bearing fruit when it wasn't even fig season. Understanding something about the features of Palestine, however, sheds light on Jesus' action. There are actually several varieties of fig trees that grow in that region, and one variety bears fruit out of season. The fact that Jesus saw a fig tree that appeared as if it would have fruit but did not allowed Jesus to use the fig tree as an object lesson. This illustrates how understanding the biblical context helps, for prophets in the Old Testament often communicated prophetic truth through sign acts, often using objects from ordinary life.

- Some consider the Apostle Paul's views about women chauvinistic. How do such accusations betray a greater dilemma over the nature and application of Scripture?

  Those who consider the Apostle Paul's views about women chauvinistic and an example of first-century prejudice feel at liberty to dismiss Paul's teaching about women and leadership in the church. This attitude betrays a low view of Scripture, that an agent of God's revelation espoused prejudiced views that are out of accord with cultural developments. It also shows the difficulty of applying the Bible to our modern situation and forces us to ask what parts of Scripture are enduring and what parts merely applied to the culture to which it was written.

- What danger is involved when considering whether something in Scripture is a principle or a custom?

  A danger arises when we are too quick to categorize something in Scripture as customary. It is a very serious offense against God to dismiss a principle that He has set down as normative for all Christians as a custom that has no bearing on us today. This does violence to the authority of God. On the other hand, to take something that God intended to be only a temporary custom and impose it on all people in every age is to do violence to the people of God.

REVIEW QUIZ

Lesson 11

1. **D.**
   Our twofold problem when studying Scripture is not only interpreting what it means but also applying it to our lives. Application is the second, and perhaps most difficult, problem we face when seeking to understand the Bible.

2. **B.**
   Apodictic laws are the moral absolutes of Scripture. As moral absolutes, they are most like the principles discussed in this lesson. Casuistic laws are the case laws of Scripture. They are based on apodictic laws and give us general guidelines for similar situations, but many of them are culturally specific, though we can learn from their general equity. Proverbial laws, while truly the wisdom of God, must be applied with wisdom to our particular situation.

3. **A.**
   When we recognize that Scripture itself contains both customs and principles, we are then faced with the sobering question about distinguishing between custom and principle. The guidelines that help us navigate this responsibility will be discussed in the next lesson.

4. **C.**
   Dr. Sproul used the example of women in the church to raise our awareness of the difficulties that can be caused when attempting to faithfully apply Scripture to the modern day. It brings up the difficult challenge of determining Scripture's relationship with culture and the question about principles and customs in Scripture.

5. **A.**
   There is danger in both scenarios. When we dismiss a principle as a custom, then we offend God and do violence to His authority. When we raise a custom to the level

of a principle, requiring that it be practiced by everyone, then we do violence to the liberty of God's people.

6. **C.**
   Dr. Sproul gave two examples of possible customary practices: Jesus' foot-washing and instruction to His disciples to do likewise and His instruction to His disciples about what not to take on mission when He sent them out in Luke 10. Jesus' institution of the Lord's Supper and His command that we continually observe it is a perpetual, enduring command.

12

Principle vs. Custom

INTRODUCTION

When we look at the various customs described throughout Scripture, how do we understand the way that they apply to the modern day? Is there deeper meaning rooted in these teachings, or are they simply cultural issues? In this lesson, Dr. Sproul provides guidelines for distinguishing between local customs and universal principles in the Bible to conclude this study on biblical interpretation.

LEARNING GOALS

When you have finished this lesson, you should be able to:

- Engage with Paul's argument in 1 Corinthians 11:2–16
- Summarize four ways of interpreting biblical practices and modern-day application
- Follow four guidelines for differentiating between custom and principle

KEY IDEAS

- When we encounter instructions and injunctions in the Bible, we must discern whether we are dealing with custom or principle.
- Covering the head is an example of a practice followed in the history of the church that has largely been abandoned, revealing divergent ways of interpreting and applying the Bible.
- The most prudent guideline for Christians to follow when distinguishing between custom and principle is to exercise humility.

REFLECTION & DISCUSSION QUESTIONS

Before the Video

What Do You Think?

Take a moment to answer the following questions. They will prepare you for the lecture.

- How has this teaching series been most helpful in enhancing your ability to engage with Scripture?

- How does our approach to studying, interpreting, and applying the Bible relate to Christian obedience?

Scripture Reading

I appeal to you, brothers, by the name of our Lord Jesus Christ, that all of you agree, and that there be no divisions among you, but that you be united in the same mind and the same judgment. For it has been reported to me by Chloe's people that there is quarreling among you, my brothers. What I mean is that each one of you says, "I follow Paul," or "I follow Apollos," or "I follow Cephas," or "I follow Christ." Is Christ divided? Was Paul crucified for you? Or were you baptized in the name of Paul?

— 1 Corinthians 1:10–13

- What does this passage reveal about a significant problem in the Corinthian church?

During the Video

Answer the following questions while you watch the video. They will guide you through the lecture.

Four Views *0:00–10:03*

- What is the first interpretation of 1 Corinthians 11:2–16?

- What is the second interpretation of 1 Corinthians 11:2–16?

- What are the third and fourth interpretations of 1 Corinthians 11:2–16? How do they relate?

Four Guidelines *10:03–28:36*

- What is the first guideline for distinguishing a principle from a custom?

- What is the second guideline for distinguishing a principle from a custom?

- What is the third guideline for distinguishing a principle from a custom?

- What is the fourth guideline for distinguishing a principle from a custom?

After the Video

Answer the following questions after you have finished the lecture. They will help you identify and summarize the major points.

- Which of the four views of 1 Corinthians 11:2–16 do you take? Why?

  If you are in a group, have the members read 1 Corinthians 11:2–16. Invite them to respond to the following questions: What are the most challenging verses to interpret in this passage? Which of the four interpretive options seems most apparent in the text?

- Read Ephesians 5:25–33. Since we know that Scripture interprets Scripture, which of the four views of 1 Corinthians 11:2–16 seems to be ruled out?

  If you are in a group, have the members compare 1 Corinthians 11:2–16; Ephesians 5:25–33; and 1 Timothy 2:8–15. Have them discuss what these passages have in common.

- Which guideline did Dr. Sproul consider the most important? Why do you think it is so important? How can you ensure that you follow it?

  If you are in a group, have the members discuss Dr. Sproul's statement in the previous lesson that it is dangerous both to reduce a principle to the level of a custom and to raise a custom to the level of a principle. How does the group reconcile this danger with the principle of humility?

PRAYER

Commit what you have learned from God's Word in this lesson to prayer.

- Praise God for the opportunity to grow in your ability to interpret Scripture.
- Confess any sins of pride and presumption over the meaning of a Scripture passage.
- Thank God that He has promised in His Word to equip you for every good work.
- Ask God to give you a greater confidence by His Spirit in handling His Word.

REVIEW QUIZ

Use these multiple-choice questions to measure what you learned from this lesson.

1. Stating that Paul argues for head coverings because of first-century prostitution practices violates which guideline for differentiating a principle from a custom?
   a. Be aware of creation principles.
   b. Examine the Bible for apparent customs.
   c. Allow for first-century Christian distinctives.
   d. Do not violate what may be a principle.
2. Which guideline explicitly suggests that 1 Corinthians 11:2–16, in some manner, concerns a principle?
   a. Be aware of creation principles.
   b. Examine the Bible for apparent customs.
   c. Allow for first-century Christian distinctives.
   d. Do not violate what may be a principle.
3. An interpretation of 1 Corinthians 11:2–16 in which head coverings are customary rejects that idea that a wife ought to submit to her husband.
   a. True
   b. False
4. Which of the following is *not* an example of a custom acknowledged by the Bible?
   a. Language
   b. Clothing styles
   c. Monetary systems
   d. Marriage standards
5. Historical research into first-century cultural practices should not be considered when interpreting the Bible.
   a. True
   b. False

6. What is the principle of humility?
    a. Be aware of creation principles.
    b. Examine the Bible for apparent customs.
    c. Allow for first-century Christian distinctives.
    d. Do not violate what may be a principle.

Answer Key—Principle vs. Custom

REFLECTION & DISCUSSION QUESTIONS

Before the Video

What Do You Think?

These are personal questions. The answers should be based on your own knowledge and experience.

Scripture Reading

- What does this passage reveal about a significant problem in the Corinthian church?

  Early in his first letter to the Corinthians, Paul addresses a significant problem in the Corinthian church, which should inform us about one of the purposes of his letter. In this passage, he addresses the divisions and factions that were being expressed by allegiances to various leaders in the early church. Throughout the letter, Paul addresses the divisions in the church in areas such as sexual practice, civil life, Christian liberty, worship, and spiritual gifts. It is important to remember Paul's emphasis on unity in this letter as you study 1 Corinthians 11:2–16 in this lesson.

During the Video

Four Views

- What is the first interpretation of 1 Corinthians 11:2–16?

  The first interpretation of 1 Corinthians 11:2–16 is that Paul is arguing for a first-century custom that has no relevance in the modern day. This view argues that wearing a head covering was only a customary way of signaling a woman's submission to her husband and that even the idea that a wife should be submissive to her husband was customary.

- What is the second interpretation of 1 Corinthians 11:2–16?

  The second interpretation of 1 Corinthians 11:2–16 is that Paul is arguing for head coverings as a pure principle. The practice of covering the head, what head coverings represent, and even the use of a veil as a head covering are all transcultural principles.

- What are the third and fourth interpretations of 1 Corinthians 11:2–16? How do they relate?

  The third and fourth interpretations of 1 Corinthians 11:2–16 are related because they are hybrid views of the first and second interpretations, blending principle and custom. The third view states that Paul is arguing for a wife's submission to her husband as a principle, whereas the practice of wearing head coverings is customary and no longer required. The fourth view states that Paul is arguing for both a wife's submission to her husband and the wearing of head coverings as principles, but that the head coverings themselves do not have to be veils. In this view, the manner in which the head is covered is customary.

Four Guidelines

- What is the first guideline for distinguishing a principle from a custom?

  The first guideline for distinguishing a principle from a custom is to examine the Bible to see whether Scripture itself acknowledges some things as customary. This principle understands that the Bible was written over a two-thousand-year period by different authors in different cultural settings, so we should expect to find local language and clothing customs, for example.

- What is the second guideline for distinguishing a principle from a custom?

  The second guideline is to allow for Christian distinctions in the first century. This means that while historical and cultural insights about first-century practices can be helpful, the Christian community did not necessarily adhere to such practices for the same reasons. We must therefore, whenever possible, look to the rationale provided in Scripture for an explanation of Christian practices.

- What is the third guideline for distinguishing a principle from a custom?

  The third guideline is to be aware of creation principles. These are the principles that God has given to all human beings as human beings. Therefore, these principles are by nature transcultural. They go all the way back to creation, so we must take notice when they are used when distinguishing a principle from a custom.

- What is the fourth guideline for distinguishing a principle from a custom?

  The fourth guideline, when one still cannot distinguishing between principle and custom after following the first three guidelines, is to be humble. It is prudent to approach the matter in question by giving it the benefit of the doubt that it is a principle.

After the Video

- Which of the four views of 1 Corinthians 11:2–16 do you take? Why?

  This question is subjective but should select from the four interpretive options provided in this lesson. These options range between viewing 1 Corinthians 11:2–16 as pure custom, pure principle, or a hybrid of principle and custom. Ultimately, the four guidelines for distinguishing principle from custom should shape your view.

- Read Ephesians 5:25–33. Since we know that Scripture interprets Scripture, which of the four views of 1 Corinthians 11:2–16 seems to be ruled out?

Ephesians 5:25–33 calls husbands to love their wives and wives to submit to their husbands. Only one of the four options for interpreting 1 Corinthians 11:2–16 views this marital dynamic as customary. Unless one were to altogether reject the application of Ephesians 5:25–33 to marriage, the first interpretation of the head-coverings passage as purely customary should be ruled out by virtue of Scripture's interpretation of Scripture.

- Which guideline did Dr. Sproul consider to be the most important? Why do you think it is so important? How can you ensure that you follow it?

  Dr. Sproul considered the fourth guideline about humility to be the most important. While you may have other reasons why it is such an important principle, Dr. Sproul stressed that whatever we do that is not of faith is sin (Rom. 14:23), so it is better for us to err on the side of obeying God when we have doubts and cannot adequately discern whether something in Scripture is a principle or a custom. There are many ways to ensure a humble frame when studying Scripture. One way is through prayer, which puts us in a posture of dependence.

REVIEW QUIZ

Lesson 12

1. **C.**
   Many scholars point to first-century customs in the Greco-Roman world to explain 1 Corinthians 11:2–16. While research in this area can be helpful, it is harmful to reject the rationale that Paul himself provides in the passage. Paul doesn't mention anything about prostitution but instead gives a different reason for the practice of head coverings. Allowing for first-century Christian distinctives helps us understand that Christians may not have practiced something for the same reasons as the culture.

2. **A.**
   In 1 Corinthians 11:2–16, Paul appeals to principles in creation to make his argument. Because of Paul's appeal to creation, we should not be quick to dismiss any one element from this passage as customary.

3. **B.**
   One interpretation of 1 Corinthians 11:2–16 rejects both head coverings as a sign and the submission of a wife to her husband as the thing signified. It is not the case, however, that a wife's submission to her husband is rejected in all interpretations that see head coverings themselves as customary. Both hybrid interpretations of this passage maintain the position that wives ought to submit to their husbands.

4. **D.**
Language, clothing styles, and currency are all examples of apparent customs in Scripture. Marriage standards are not. This would go against the third guideline for distinguishing principle from custom because the standards for marriage were established at creation.

5. **B.**
Historical studies into the cultural practices of the first century are not bad in themselves. Yet they can mislead us if first-century Christian distinctives are not considered or when the rationale provided explicitly in Scripture is ignored.

6. **D.**
While following each of the four guidelines for distinguishing principle from custom involves a measure of humility, the humility principle is the fourth guideline. When in doubt, we must not reduce what may be a principle to the level of a custom.